B.S.A.
and
LINCOLN JEFFRIES
AIR RIFLES

Three BSA military pattern air rifles stacked in the familiar 'piled arms' position representing the famous BSA trade mark

B.S.A.
and
LINCOLN JEFFRIES
AIR RIFLES

By

JOHN KNIBBS

A Concise Illustrated History
of their Development and Manufacture
1904-1918

Illustrations by Gilbert Kerry

© JOHN KNIBBS, 1986

First edition 1986

Published by
JOHN KNIBBS PUBLICATIONS
GILLIA, BLACKFIRS LANE,
BIRMINGHAM B37 7JE, U.K.

Printed in England by
ADAMS & SONS (Printers) LTD.,
Burcott Road, Hereford.

ISBN 0 9511317 0 2

Foreword

AS A collector, shooter and devotee of BSA airguns, I am particularly delighted to introduce a book in which I have especial faith. The story of Lincoln Jeffries's underlever-cocking air rifle, and the subsequent involvement of BSA (unfortunately to the detriment of the inventor) is the cornerstone of the modern British airgun industry.

Though only about eighty thousand guns were made before the First World War, their reputation was such that they were soon in the vanguard. The contemporary trade periodical *Arms & Explosives* waxed lyrical; its influential 'Lectures to Young Gunmakers' but one of the series that rightly held the Lincoln Jeffries Pattern as the highpoint of contemporary aurgunnery.

Production by Britain's premier military gunmaker undoubtedly gave the Lincoln Jeffries Pattern an important advantage denied to rivals—like the Britannia—that deserved better fates. But BSA's involvement also assured robustness, a survival rate to delight the modern collector, and an unusually good performance: my Improved Model D—dating from 1913, I learned from this book—will still outshoot many newer rackmates.

BSA has had a chequered, convoluted history. Several times rebuilt, and bombed to partial destruction in 1940, the Small Heath factory nonetheless contains sufficient material for John Knibbs to recreate those pre-1914 days when sale of airguns contributed so greatly to BSA's salvation. His dedicated, painstaking work, and unrivalled practical experience, advances not only the story of BSA but also the entire cause of British airgun scholarship.

So who should care? At a time when too much of the old, inaccuarate but well established story is simply being repeated uncritically, airgun enthusiasts should **all** be thankful that *BSA and Lincoln Jeffries Air Rifles, A Concise Illustrated History of their Development and Manufacture 1904-18* achieves so much.

John Walter
Harrow, 1986

To Pauline

Preface
By the Grandson of George Lincoln Jeffries

I have read this book, and find it an interesting and informative record of the development of the Lincoln Air Rifle, which was designed and manufactured and patented by my Grandfather the late George Lincoln Jeffries.

Research into the early design of the Air Rifle and its later production by the Birmingham Small Arms Company, has taken Mr. J. Knibbs seven years hard work, and he is to be congratulated on the excellence of this manuscript.

Lincoln George Jeffries
BIRMINGHAM, 1986

Acknowledgements

AS WITH any new reference work, it is not possible to correlate any worthwhile information without depending on the help and guidance provided by other knowledgeable collectors and researchers. In this respect I am greatly indebted to the enormous help and assistance given to me by Gilbert Kerry who, next to myself, is the most ardent of *"Besasphiles"* whose enthusiasm and knowledge of all things BSA have encouraged me through the more arduous preparation of this work. His superb photographs reproduced in the following pages highlight another of his several talents. Many of the rifles illustrated are from his own private collection.

I would also like to thank the Directors and Staff of BSA Guns Limited of Birmingham for their patience and advice so freely given. The Proof Master of Birmingham Gun Barrel Proof House for allowing me access to trade records, patents etc., Hugh Earl of Pax Guns of London for his help and loan of many guns from his extensive collection. John Walter for his invaluable assistance throughout my researches and help in getting into print. Eddie Barber for photographs of the Gun Laying Teacher and my many friends in the Birmingham Gun Trade and the many collectors throughout the world, particularly Dr. Trevor Morris and his colleague Trevor Adams in New Zealand, who have supplied many details of weapons in their collections.

Mr. Lincoln George Jeffries has been most helpful and very patient with me and has contributed greatly to the clarification of historical events related to his family. I also acknowledge the kind assistance given to me by the curator and staff of the Pattern Room, Enfield Lock, Middlesex.

Finally, I thank my wife Pauline, who has so readily and uncomplainingly typed and retyped endless notes and manuscripts for the last seven years. It is to her, with my love, that this book is dedicated.

JOHN KNIBBS,
BIRMINGHAM, ENGLAND.
1986.

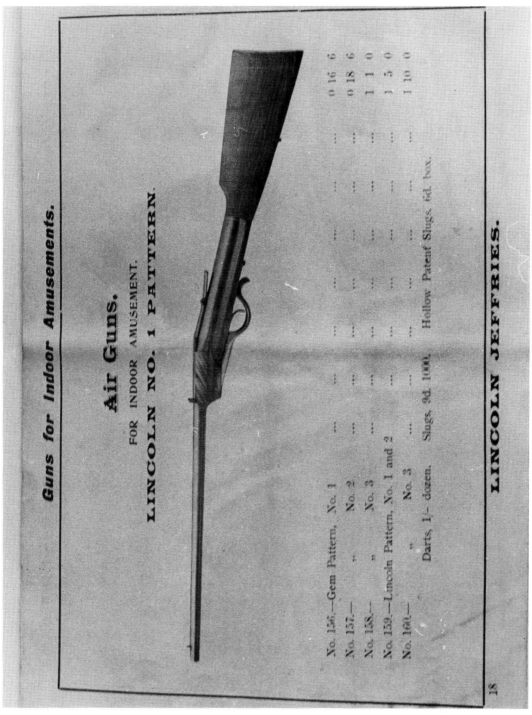

PLATE 1 *(G. Kerry)*
The range of Lincoln Air Rifles and Guns available 1905.

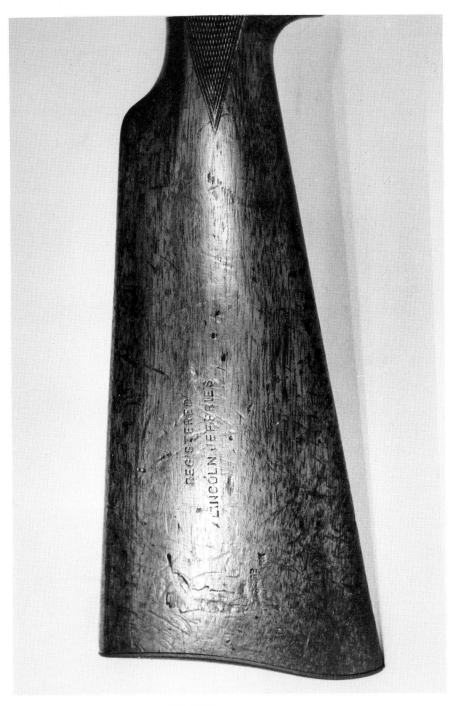

PLATE 2 *(G. Kerry)*
Stock marking of First Pattern Lincoln Air Rifles.
This design was registered on 14th January, 1904, Registered Number 260142.

PLATE 3 *(G. Kerry)*
BSA 'Piled Arms' Trade Mark.

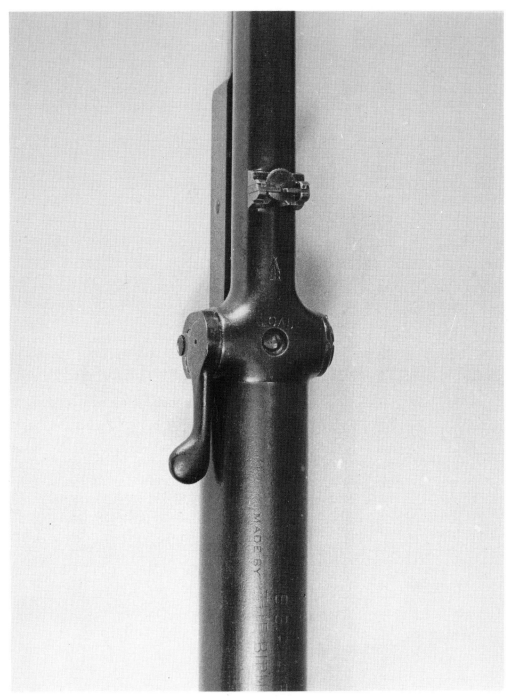

PLATE 4 *(G. Kerry)*
Details of the First Pattern Breech Plug fitted to BSA and Lincoln Air Rifles.
Top view.

BSA and LINCOLN JEFFRIES AIR RIFLES 1904-1918

Chapter 1

THE BSA AIR rifle, with its fixed barrel, separate cocking lever and rotary pellet loading breech plug is probably the best known model throughout the world. In the eighty or more years since its development, the basic design is still used by BSA in the Airsporter models and the unique cocking and loading system is adopted by most major air weapon manufacturers today. One has only to glance at the Webley & Scott Mark III, Osprey and Tracker, Original Model 50, Relum Tornado and some of the Air Arms range to see the basic design still in operation. Even some of the so called revolutionary air weapon designs such as the BSA Merlin, ASI Paratrooper Repeater and even the latest Weihrauch Model HW 77, all incorporate some part of the original ideas from which the BSA Air Rifle was conceived at the turn of this century.

The one man responsible for the enormous advance made to air weapon design and development was Mr. Lincoln Jeffries whose genius and enterprise in the field of Air Rifle technology can be equated with that of the Wright Brothers in aviation and Marconi in the field of telecommunications.

Born in 1847, the son of George Jeffries, Gunmaker of Norwich in Norfolk, Lincoln Jeffries worked with his brother in his father's business in Orford Hill, Norwich until 1866 when, at the age of nineteen, he came to Birmingham and obtained employment in the Gun Trade with several skilled outworkers. By 1873, Lincoln Jeffries had established himself in the Gun Trade in his own right and his name appears on the Birmingham Trade Register of that year at an address of 31 Whittall Street. His main business was the manufacture and repair of sporting guns which at that period were in the heyday of their development. In 1888, larger premises were found in the same street at number 48 and ten years later, business had improved to such an extent that he moved to larger premises still, at 121 Steelhouse Lane in the heart of the gunmaking quarter of the City of Birmingham. By the end of the century, Lincoln Jeffries' business was well established and as well as producing a range of hammer and hammerless shotguns under the Company name, there was also being made several types of air canes with both rifled and smoothbored barrels in both breech loading and muzzle loading versions. The Company also produced air pumps, ram rods and bullets for these air weapons.

Following the lead of many other small gun manufacturers in Birmingham, a range of break barrel type air guns were also included in the Lincoln Jeffries' catalogue, produced in 1900. These air guns were offered in three calibres. No. 1, 2 and 3, all with smoothbored barrels, some of which were identical to the Haviland and Gunn Gem Type air guns of the period (see Plate 1). Other models were of the Millita type introduced in 1901, being simple break barrel models with side catch locking and a cast cocking lever and separate trigger guard. Although marketed under the Lincoln Jeffries name, all these air guns appeared to be of basic foreign manufacture with minor improvements and embellishments carried out by the importer/distributor. Darts in all three calibres and slugs were also offered by Lincoln Jeffries and Company. As the firm produced bullets for air canes, it is possible that the air gun slugs were of Birmingham manufacture and not imported.

The practice of importing finished air guns from America and Germany and carrying out minimal modifications before marking them with the names of famous British Gunmakers importing the weapons was very widespread at the end of the nineteenth century and in fact was condemned by the trade journals of the day. This practice was rife even in the prodigious London Gun Trade. It was soon found that higher prices could be asked for cheap air guns, even if they were only slightly different than the original imported model if they bore a famous British name. Most importers fitted improved mainsprings and some also supplied improved locking catches to the barrels or fitted modified sights. At that time, any alteration to the original was considered justification for renaming the article and offering it for sale as London or Birmingham made. Lincoln Jeffries was no exception to this deception as an air gun offered as '‛H' The Lincoln Air Rifle' in the first year of this century was almost identical to the German produced Millita air guns available in calibres of No. 1, No. 2 and N. 3 bore, the "Lincoln" designated models had modified locking catches and probably straighter barrels and better quality springs than cheaper other models. Most of his guns had rifled barrels, most probably supplied by the German manufacturers, although Lincoln Jeffries did claim to be "The Inventor of Rifling the Modern Air Gun" on his letterheads of the period.

Immediately after the Boer or South African War, there was a great revival in target shooting in Britain. This new interest was encouraged by the Government of the day who were only too conscious of the abysmal marksmanship of the average British soldier compared to the superb performance of the Boer Commando Troops with their advanced Mauser repeating rifles, the use of which completely altered modern warfare and encouraged the development of more accurate rifles for the British Forces. Efforts had been made by the War Office to equip the Army with a better weapon than the single shot Martini Henry Rifle introduced in 1871. The Lee-Enfield Long Pattern Bolt Action Repeating rifle in .303 calibre had been supplied to the British South African Army and although basically the weapon was up to the standard of German Mauser rifles, the Lee-Enfield's sights were very inferior, and more importantly, the individual marksmanship of the average British soldier was incredibly poor.

Until the Boer War, the British Army had fought on a pre-determined communal basis, firing mass volleys into a co-operative enemy, also drawn up in neat ranks within rifle shot. In South Africa, the Boer forces consisted mainly of farmers who had been trained in the use of the rifle even before they were old enough to ride. Greatly outnumbered, they used their stalking and hunting skills combined with their inborn marksmanship, to hold the whole British Expeditionary Army at bay and eventually force the British into Peace Negotiations.

The skill of the Boers in partisan and commando type tactics and particularly accurate rifle shooting had not gone unnoticed in Whitehall. Encouragement was given to Public School Cadet Forces, Boys Brigades, Working Mens Clubs etc. to ease up on the drill and military manoeuvres and concentrate more on perfecting rifle marksmanship. Shooting skills were fostered at all levels and many factories had rifle ranges as part of their sports facilities. During the summer months, practice could be had with small bore cartridge rifles built on the now obsolete Martini Henry actions of unwanted military rifles. These rifles were chambered for the .297/.230 long or short Morris tube cartridge or the newly developed .22 long rifle rim fire cartridge. Rifles and ammunition in these calibres were expensive to buy, noisy and required specially constructed ranges for their safe usage.

The airgun was the ideal weapon for cheap, safe, quiet shooting training. The air guns of the day, however, as already described, were not capable of producing the accuracy required for serious target shooting. It was in an endeavour to improve target accuracy that some of the modifications already mentioned, were undertaken by British Gunmakers.

By 1903, Lincoln Jeffries was offering his "Lincoln" air rifles as "the most accurate air gun sold". Still the Millita Type of design but with professionally straightened rifled barrel, new sights and "specially designed for Club type shooting". "Clubs who desire to become proficient in their shooting", were advised to use Lincoln Jeffries guns; which were "guaranteed to average 20 points by even indifferent shots". At what range and under what conditions were not specified. The target air guns were also advertised as being able to "kill birds at 18 yards". In the same advertisement, mention was made that "air guns could be re-sighted". Mr. Lincoln Jeffries could at this time foresee the great potential for the air gun if it's construction could be improved.

Whether the availability of more accurate air guns led to the great increase in Shooting Clubs or whether the increase in Clubs increased the demand for more accurate air guns is debateable. One thing, however, is certain, in the first few years of King Edward VII's reign, there were active and growing Air Gun Shooting Clubs in most towns and villages throughout the Kingdom. In Birmingham, air guns shooting was a sufficiently popular sport to justify its own separate column in the Sports page of the local newspaper. A National Air Rifle Association was formed with its headquarters in Birmingham and many gunmaking companies were now becoming interested in supplying equipment for the new sport. A whole array of targets and target holders blossomed forth as did a wide range of air gun pellets and slugs. Some slugs were even produced with angled fins to impart a spinning action when fired in smoothbored air guns. Replacement mainsprings were also advertised; even a short lived spring of square section wire was manufactured by A. B. Williams & Co. Ltd., of 13 Weaman Street, Birmingham. This spring was actually marketed under the name of "The Club". Air guns were now being produced with rifled barrels, foremost amongst which were the Mayer & Grammelspacker Diana and the Langenbau Millita imported by Martin Pulversman & Co. of London.

During these early days, Lincoln Jeffries had confirmed to himself that even with extensive and often expensive, modifications, the break barrel air guns and rifles on the market were just not capable of producing the high, consistent, accurate shooting demanded by Airgun Clubs. He had the foresight and gunmaking experience to look at the problems, not in terms of modifications to inadequate designs, but in terms of

17

a completely new design of air gun.

The main problem to be overcome was the efficient air sealing of the breech. Having produced both muzzle and breech loading air canes, Lincoln Jeffries appreciated that the key factor in accurate shooting was efficient breech closure and this was achieved more effectively with muzzle loading than with breech loading air canes. He had for several years been experimenting with a fixed barrel design of air rifle with various designs of sliding or rotary breech mechanisms. By far the most satisfactory was a rotary breech plug system based on the common gas tap design. His premises were next door but one to Felix Bateman & Co. Gasfitters, so he would have been familiar with the excellent sealing property of this gas control system.

Between 1901 and 1904, Mr. Lincoln Jeffries manufactured a quantity of various prototype models. Following a practice still current in the Gun Trade, much of the basic manufacturing work was given to outworkers specialising in particular engineering skills. Although his factory premises were in the Birmingham Gun Trade, much of his experimental work was put out to non Gun Trade businesses and there is evidence that a proportion of the actual manufacturing work was carried out in the Kidderminster/ Bromsgrove area in the adjacent County of Worcestershire. It is possible that this work was deliberately kept out of the Birmingham Trade to ensure secrecy of any development work and to prevent any successful ideas being poached by fellow Gunmakers. All the designs of fixed barrel rifles were cocked by means of an articulated lever positioned under the barrel. Of those early rifles examined, the rotary loading taps were of very narrow section, traversing completely the breech section of the rifle; held in position by a large headed screw over a large diameter washer or collar. The operating lever for the tap was on the right hand side of the rifle. As these models were all hand made, the fitting of the parts was excellent and the rifles were very accurate. For identification purposes, the experimental rifles were serial numbered with the prefix letter 'H' which was to be used on the rifle logo of all standard length rifles manufactured by or for Lincoln Jeffries up to November 1913 when the last 'H' The Lincoln Air Rifle was despatched. Serial numbers seen on two of these early experimental rifles were H79 and H29. Mr. Lincoln Jeffries had used the prefix letter 'H' when marking his Gem and Millita modified models. The significance of the letter 'H' is unclear. It has been suggested that it identified the standard or "Heavy" Pattern rifles. This however is unlikely as at that time there were three calibres of rifle available and the Ladies or 'L' pattern air rifle was still several years away. It is suggested that the letter 'H' was based on the Lincoln Jeffries registered trade name of "Hercules" used by the family business to cover the gun repair and welding side of the trade.

With possibly just over 100 of these new fixed barrel rifles sold and proving very successful in competition circles, it was clearly evident that the small manufacturing company in Steelhouse Lane could not possibly cope with the demand which this new design had created.

Lincoln Jeffries firstly, very wisely, applied for a patent to protect his new design of an air rifle with fixed barrel and breech and an under lever system for cocking and this was granted on 12th March, 1904 and allocated number 8761. Patents were also taken out in Belgium and Germany; the two countries at that time producing the most competition to the British Gun Trade. He then approached several of the large manufacturing companies in Birmingham with a view to the manufacture of his new rifle, either under licence or by mutual financial agreement. He had little reaction to his proposals until his approach to The Birmingham Small Arms Co. Ltd. in Small Heath, five miles away from Steelhouse Lane, resulted in quite interesting and promising responses.

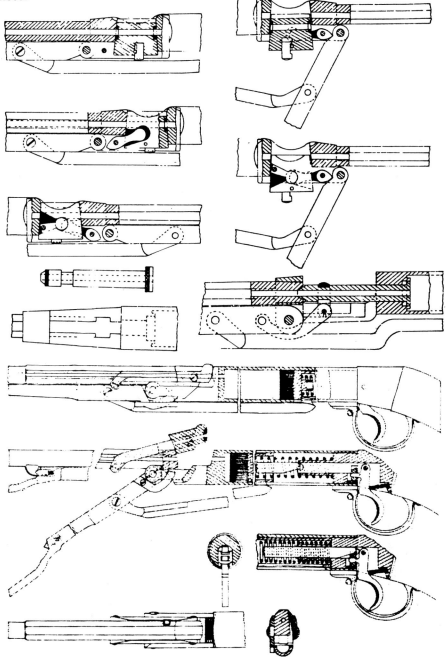

Patent 8761 of 1905. Part drawings, first part. Lincoln Jeffries.

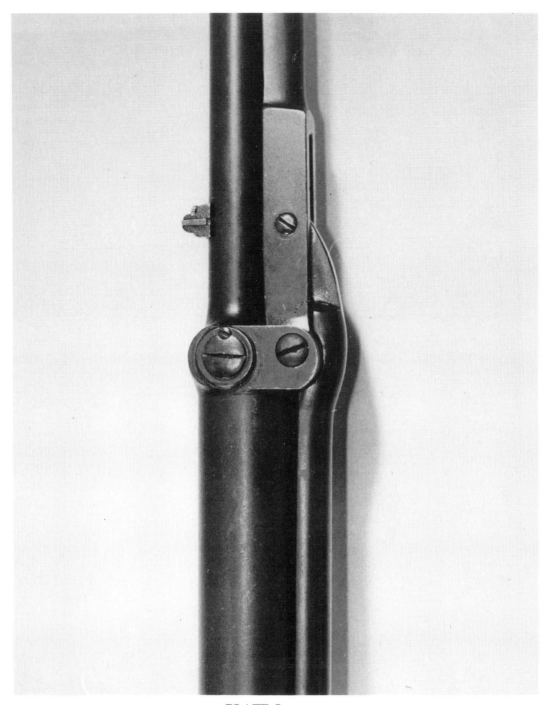

PLATE 5 *(G. Kerry)*
Details of the First Pattern Breech Plug fitted to BSA and Lincoln Rifles.
Right hand side view.

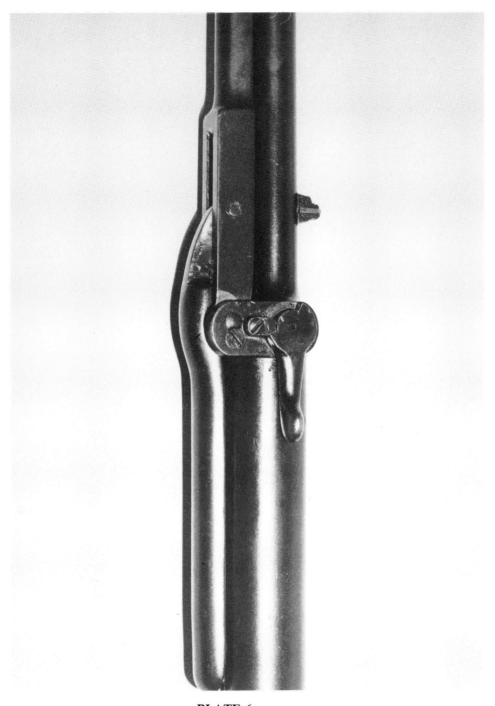

PLATE 6 *(G. Kerry)*
Details of the First Pattern Breech Plug fitted to BSA and Lincoln Air Rifles.
Left hand side view.

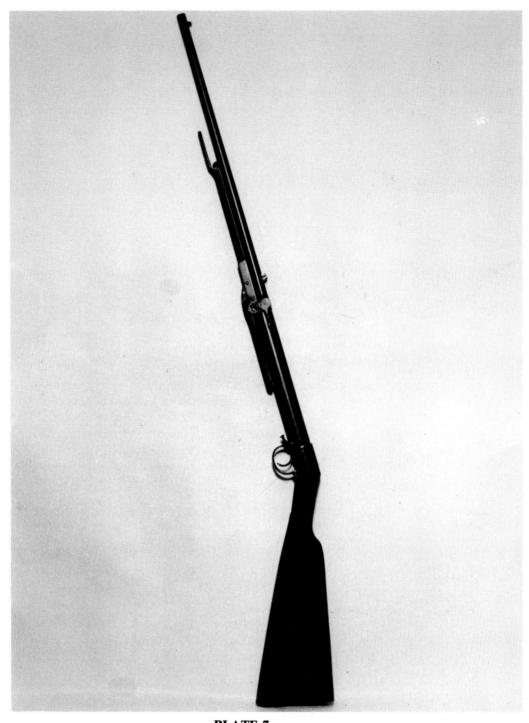

PLATE 7 *(G. Kerry)*
First Pattern 'H The Lincoln Air Rifle'.

Chapter 2

THE BIRMINGHAM Small Arms Company Limited was formed in 1861 by a number of large arms manufacturers in the Birmingham area to regulate and consolidate the supply of military arms for Government contracts and to develop the use of modern machinery in their production. A new factory was built at Small Heath, on the then outskirts of Birmingham, on a 25 acre site purchased by the new company. A new road, Armoury Road, in which the present day BSA factory is still situated, was built to link the new factory with the Great Western railway station of Small Heath. Several courts of small family houses were built along one side of Armoury Road to accommodate factory workers.

Initially, orders for military weapons were difficult to obtain; probably due to the unproven track record of the new company. The first major Government contract was granted five years after the Company's formation in 1866 for the conversion of 100,000 muzzle loading muskets to the Snider Breech Loading System. The Company, with the assistance of a previously unheard of night shift, was able to produce conversions at the rate of 3,000 per week, which proved beyond question, the superiority of a modern mechanised, automated factory compared to the inefficient and unreliable sub-contracting system in vogue in the arms industry at that period.

In 1871, a further 70,000 rifles were converted to the Snider system after which contracts were very few and far between whilst the British Government were considering the adoption of the Martini Henry single shot rifle for military usage.

In 1873, the BSA Company Ltd., purchased the nearby Adderley Park Rolling Mills to enable them to fulfil an order for 40,000,000 11 mm cartridge cases for the Prussian Government. This Company later produced the Adder Diablo Air Rifle pellet marketed by BSA. Contracts were very scarce for the next few years and in 1878, the Company shut altogether due to lack of contracts and after remaining closed for over one year, the factory reopened in 1879 in order to produce the Otto Bicycle, whose inventor impressed the board of directors by riding the new bicycle across the boardroom table several times before pedalling it down the office stairs and proceeding at a reckless pace into Birmingham city centre; which on the cobbled streets of the day must have been a very uncomfortable sales demonstration.

Between 1886 and 1900, Government orders were sporadic and several models of service rifle were made; the Enfield Martini, Martini Henry Mk. 2, Lee-Metford Mk. 1 and

2. The Lee-Enfield rifle was made in quantity in 1896 when 40,000 were delivered to the War Office, due to the demand created by the South African War. A final 41,400 Lee-Enfield Mark 2 rifles were ordered after which Government orders declined and BSA were forced to sell off the Adderley Park Rolling Mills to Nobel Explosives Ltd. This became the Birmingham Metal and Munitions Company which was to produce so much small arms ammunition during the Great War of 1914-18.

The Birmingham Small Arms Company Ltd., in mid 1904, was in a very delicate financial state. The South African Wars were over, the vast British Empire was at peace, there was no prospect of further orders from the British, or any other, major Government and one of the largest arms plants in the Empire was looking about for business.

The visit of Mr. Lincoln Jeffries with his prototype fixed barrel air rifle would, during the normal course of events, have been quickly and unceremoniously dealt with; however, due to the very depressed state of BSA at that time, it would appear that the Lincoln Jeffries proposals received eager attention from the Board who were literally scratching around for business to keep the work force at Small Heath employed.

The prospect of the production of an air rifle which was entirely outside the scope of BSA's military work, did show that Mr. Lincoln Jeffries had been able to convince the Company's Board of Directors that his new design of air rifle, if manufactured with the same care and precision as that required for the production of military weapons, could raise the image of the air rifle from that of a nursery toy to that of a useful aid to marksmanship. Air rifle shooting with a well made, accurate air rifle could encourage many people to take an interest in rifle shooting generally, which could result ultimately in increased sales of BSA rifles and guns.

In the early part of 1905, a contract was signed between Mr. Lincoln Jeffries and The Birmingham Small Arms Company Ltd., whereby the Company would undertake to produce an air rifle to Mr. Jeffries design to be sold by him under his name and under the Lincoln Jeffries trade mark of the shooting man (see Plate 2). At the time of signing, it was also agreed between the parties that BSA would also market a version of Mr. Jeffries' rifle under their own name and trade mark of the Piled Arms (see Plate 3).

The BSA factory at that time was set up to manufacture military rifles on a mass produced basis so it was a fairly inexpensive and simple matter to adapt some of the machinery for the purpose of producing the new air rifle. Machined components presented no problem and such items as trigger blocks, triggers, sight parts and even piston bodies were easily produced at Small Heath. Cocking levers, cocking links, loading taps and some trigger guards were also forged in the BSA factory. The stock bolt was modified from a Lee-Enfield component and the screws used were either Enfield type thread sizes or BSA cycle thread sizes, many based on the old Otto bicycle screws. Initially, and in order to at least produce some rifles for sale and to take advantage of the interest and demand created by the publicity given to the new patent design of rifle, a certain amount of improvisation took place. For example, stock butts produced by Lincoln Jeffries for his Langenham break barrel air rifle modifications were used for some of the very early production. Likewise, pistons, piston washers, fixing screws and even springs were also used which were not of either companies manufacture but which happened to be available at the time in Lincoln Jeffries' warehouse stock.

The small Lincoln Jeffries works in Steelhouse Lane were more able to undertake skilled hand fitting and finishing work. This fact is confirmed by the excellent fit and finish of early 'H' The Lincoln air rifles still in existence. In order to avoid any duplication of serial numbers, an allocation system of numbering was agreed between the two companies who initially were each to make 1,000 rifles under their own individual brand names. Lincoln Jeffries had produced over 100 air rifles under his 'Lincoln' name prior to the alliance with BSA, so in order to avoid any possibility of confusion over BSA warranty covering components or products of their manufacture, it was decided to commence the numbering system for the first batch for Lincoln Jeffries at number 130.

The very early one hundred or so experimental rifles of Lincoln Jeffries own manufacture had several features which the BSA designers, particularly the Chief Production Designer, Mr. A. M. H. Driver, could see required improvement if the rifle was to withstand hard usage. Mr. Driver's experience in the design of Military weapons did much to improve the performance and facilitate the manufacture of the new air rifle commercially.

In the Lincoln Jeffries early rifles, the loading tap, or breech plug operating lever, as already stated, was on the right hand side of the rifle. This, in practice, was awkward for a normal right handed shooter to use, so the design was amended to reverse the loading tap lever position. Due to limited engineering facilities, the barrel/cylinder assembly of the experimental rifles was made in three parts; the barrel, breech and cylinder. These were then screwed together. Inevitably, there was an air loss from these threaded unions and Mr. Driver could see the saving in assembly time and the production of a better quality unit by forging and drawing down the barrel and breech as one unit on the same presses that produced military rifle barrel forgings.

A patent for this process was immediately applied for and was granted on 11th January, 1906 (Patent 11817 (1905)). These forged barrel/breech units were used for all the early BSA/Lincoln production which were all marked with the BSA Piled Arms Trade Mark between the rear sight dovetail and the breech. Both Lincoln and BSA air rifles from hereon were also marked in a similar fashion.

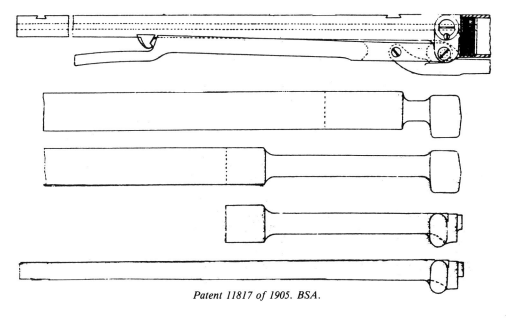

Patent 11817 of 1905. BSA.

A patent was also taken out by BSA to cover the reversed loading tap lever and an improved method of fixture in the breech. Patent Granted in 1906 (see Plate 4). A dished spring washer was fitted to the right hand side of the breech plug. This had a cut away segment to accommodate a small keeper screw which locked the large headed retaining screw to the dished washer. The washer had a square, central hole which fitted exactly over the square protruding end of the breech plug. Wear on the breech plug could be compensated by turning the large under screw washer through 90° and tightening the fixing screw ¼ of a turn to lock it into position (see Plate 5).

By the Summer of 1905, the first thousand 'H The Lincoln' air rifles were delivered to Lincoln Jeffries & Co. Ltd. at 121 Steelhouse Lane. They were in an almost complete state, requiring only minimal fitting of loading taps, sights etc. The BSA Board were obviously very interested in the reception these new type of air rifles would receive from the British Shooting public. Not having had any previous experience in this end of the arms market, they were anxious to see how sales progressed with the Lincoln Air Rifle before commencing manufacture under their own Brand Name. In May, 1905, the National Air Rifle Association established an armoury at its headquarters in Imperial Arcade in Birmingham. Its object was to display to members of clubs, samples of pellets, targets, target holders and, of course, air rifles. Rifles were on display from Mr. C. G. Bonehill (The Britannia), E. Anson (The Ansonia) and Mr. Lincoln Jeffries (The Lincoln) (see Plate 7). The shooting clubs were, therefore, aware of the new fixed barrel design and could see the several improvements over the conventional break-barrel models on display.

PLATE 8 *(G. Kerry)*
Early Pattern Long Tang Trigger Guards fitted to:
Left—straight hand stock models and Right—pistol hand stock models.

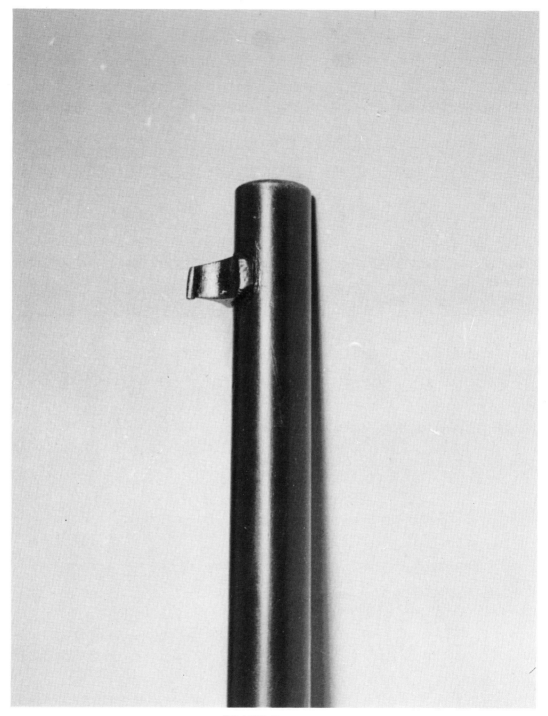

PLATE 9 *(G. Kerry)*
Details of First Pattern Foresight with bead as fitted to the BSA Air Rifle and Lincoln Models.

PLATE 10 *(G. Kerry)*
Cylinder marking on Ladies Pattern Lincoln Air Rifle from the seventh batch of
Lincoln Air Rifles.

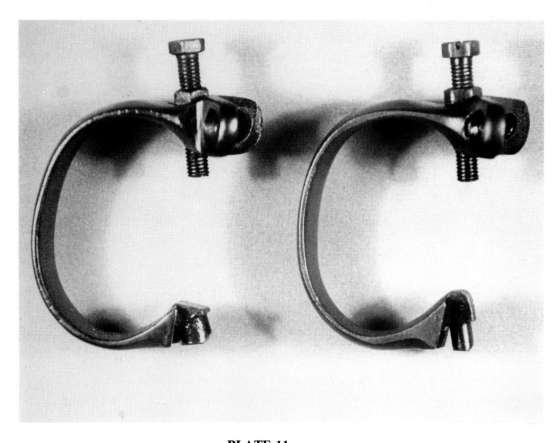

PLATE 11 *(G. Kerry)*
Left—Trigger Guard with enlarged location stud or peg as fitted to Improved Model D.
Right—Trigger Guard with small diameter location stud or peg as fitted to the BSA Improved
Model and Improved Model B.

Chapter 3

THE FIRST batch of 1,000 rifles delivered to Lincoln Jeffries Steelhouse Lane address, were serial numbered from 130 to 1129. They were all in .177 (No. 1 Bore) calibre and were all of the same pattern as regards length. Two styles of stocks were offered. The Pistol Hand version gave the rifle a total weight of 7 lbs. and a Straight Hand model weighed 6 lbs. 14 ozs.

The barrel was tapered towards the muzzle and measured 19¼″ in length. The bore was rifled with a shallow polygroove rifling developed by BSA specially for the new air rifle and still used by the company at the present time, which accounts for the very accurate air rifle barrels on current BSA models.

The breech block, as stated, was an integral part of the forged barrel and the seamless drawn tube cylinder was screwed and soldered in position on the rear of the block which was drilled and reemed transversely to receive the tapered loading tap or breech plug. This plug had a long, elegant operating lever on the left side and was retained in position from the narrow or right hand side by means of a large washer fitting over a square projection on the plug body. The washer was fixed by a large headed screw and small keeper screw. The keeper was to secure the large headed screw to the washer preventing any looseness during operation of the barrel plug assembly. The outer edge of the lever end of the plug was recessed for one quarter of its circumference and the plug movement was limited through an arc of 90° by a peg screwed to the breech block which fitted in this recess (see Plate 6). The plug was drilled across its width to form the pellet chamber which was in line with the operating lever. When the lever was in the raised or upright position, the pellet chamber was exposed for loading and when in the horizontal or closed position, the chamber was in line with the bore.

The rifle was cocked by means of an articulated two piece lever system. The hand lever was 12″ long, pivoted between two trunnions machined in the breech under the breech plug. The 7″ cocking link was pivoted on the hand lever just in front of the axis pin. The rear of the link had a stud which worked inside a slot machined in the underside of the cylinder and connected directly with the piston. The forward end of the hand lever was cranked and flattened into a duck's bill shape to effect a hand hold, the upper surface of which was chequered to give an effective grip. The cocking linkage was retained in position under the barrel by a spring operating plunger which engaged onto a catch fitted to the underside of the barrel.

The trigger block was fastened to the stock by a large headed stout bolt running through the centre of the stock. This bolt was adapted from a Lee-Enfield component as were the two fixing screws which fixed the pressed steel butt plate in position.

The trigger and sear was of one piece construction, hinged in the trigger block with a single screw. Three grooves were cut in the curve of the trigger to give non-slip finger control. The trigger was spring loaded to ensure positive engagement in the bent of the piston rod.

The air piston was machined from a casting and had the piston rod screwed into the head, locked in position by a keeper screw. The one piece leather piston washer was retained on the piston head with a large headed screw. It is interesting to note that this piston washer retaining screw was of the same thread size and type as the two trigger guard front fixing screws; the piston rod keeper screw and the rearsight bar elevating screw. The thread was a BSA bicycle/Otto bicycle size of 37 threads to the inch. This thread size was exploited by BSA in later advertising literature and was proclaimed as a specially developed thread for air rifle sight screws!

The one piece mainspring consisted of 40 coils of oval section wire fitted over a piston rod guide tube which was screwed and soldered into the front of the trigger block.

The trigger guard of the Lincoln rifle was of cast construction and was probably either made by Lincoln Jeffries or by a small sub-contractor in the Birmingham Trade. It was untypically rough in finish. The front end of the bow was flaired out to accommodate a pair of retaining screws which served the double purpose of also locking the trigger block to the cylinder. The rear of the trigger guard had a long tang which fitted into a groove cut in the hand of the stock (see Plate 8). The tang was fixed by a dome headed wood screw, many examples of early Lincoln rifles have this screw missing or replaced as it was very short in length due to the stock fixing bolt which was only a quarter of an inch or so under the wood of the stock. The front of the bow of the trigger guard was drilled and tapped for the trigger weight adjusting screw which was locked in position by a hexagonal nut.

The foresight was of the bead type and was fitted into a dovetail in the barrel. The sight had overhanging shoulders to give added rigidity but these prevented it being locked into position following any windage adjustment (see Plate 9). The rearsight was very complicated for an air rifle fitment. It consisted of a base block dovetailed into the barrel forward of the breech plug. This block accepted a flat blade or bar which could be raised or lowered for elevation adjustment by means of a domed headed knurled screw. Adjustment for windage was only possible by moving the complete rearsight laterally in its barrel dovetail. An interesting feature was a "butterfly" leaf spring underneath the elevating screw. This spring controlled and stabilised the tension of adjustment. This spring, more often than not, is found to be missing due to its fragile nature being constructed of very thin gauge sheet steel.

Samples of this first batch of Lincoln air rifles can be identified by their serial number stamped on the left side of the trigger block above the trigger. The right hand face of the walnut stock is impressed with Lincoln Jeffries Air Rifle trade mark of a Man shooting a Gun above the inscription:

"Lincoln Jeffries, Inventor and Patentee
121 Steelhouse Lane,
Birmingham."

The Trade Mark used by Mr. Lincoln Jeffries for his other rifles and shotguns was in the form of a bowler hatted marksman shooting in the prone position. Above the figure were the words "The Rifle held Straight is England's Strength". The top of the air cylinder is impressed with the following marking:

"H THE LINCOLN AIR RIFLE PATENT"

Manufactured by the BSA Co. Ltd., Birmingham.

Lincoln Jeffries produced a simple folding instruction leaflet with posed photographs demonstrating how to cock and load his new air rifle. This leaflet was supplied with each rifle as was a special combination pellet pusher/seater and spanner to adjust the trigger pull and to seat the pellet firmly into the breech plug chamber.

As this first batch of rifles was all hand finished and the loading taps or breech plugs were fitted by Lincoln Jeffries before despatch, they all performed very well; their performance in the target field was far in excess of that previously obtained with any other spring powered air weapon and was a major factor in the immediate success of the new style of air rifle.

The Lincoln rifle was demonstrated at the Bisley Meeting in the summer of 1905 where there was for the first time, an airgun competition on a special range. A Bisley champion shot, Corporal Roberts of the 1st Volunteer Batallion, Royal Warwickshire Regiment, was persuaded to use the new air rifle and he put seven shots into a 1″ bull at 20 yards, making a group of $^7/_{16}″$. He also demonstrated the rifle before King Edward VII when he scored four bulls and one inner also at 20 yards. The King pronounced the new rifle "very ingenious". At the same Bisley meeting, many other shooters had the opportunity of firing the new rifle and some very acceptable groups were produced at ranges of up to 50 yards.

A rifle capable of such accurate performance was, of course, immediately accepted by the shooting public who attended that Bisley meeting but getting the new rifle demonstrated to, and eventually accepted by, the general public as a whole was a more daunting task. It is noticeable in the sporting literature of 1905, that although the Trade publications were kept fully aware of the Lincoln Jeffries air rifle developments, no publicity or advertising was undertaken by the company which did suggest a lack of funds for such purposes. We shall see later how differently the BSA version of the Lincoln air rifle was launched and promoted and how this greater marketing effort established the BSA model to the detriment of Mr. Lincoln Jeffries' "Lincoln" rifle.

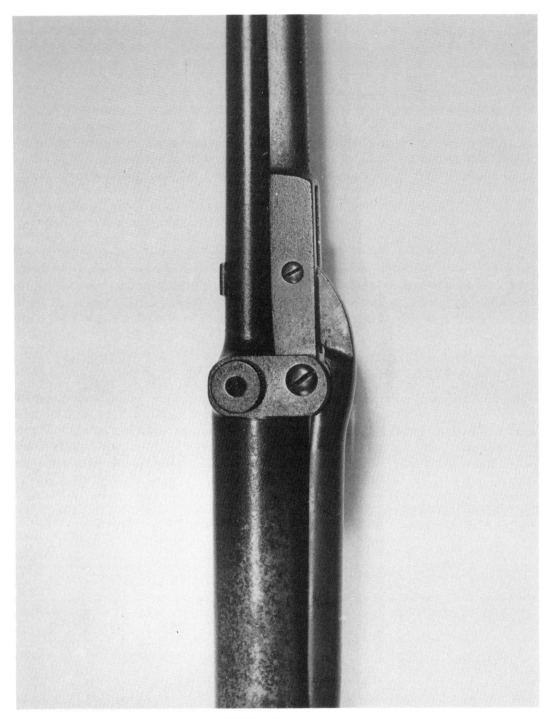

PLATE 12 *(G. Kerry)*
Details of patented Breech Plug Fastening on seventh batch of Lincoln Air Rifles.

PLATE 13 *(G. Kerry)*
Improved Breech Plug and Retaining Plate with Central Tension Spring.
Patent 8246/06, 22nd November, 1906.

PLATE 14 *(G. Kerry)*
Details of improved Breech Plugs and Retaining Plates.
Early Pattern (top) Late Pattern (bottom).

Chapter 4

AT THE September Annual General Meeting of the Birmingham Small Arms Company, the Chairman announced the commencement of manufacture of an air rifle of a pattern believed by them to be the most efficient on the market. He hoped that this branch of trade would be a permanent and lucrative one.

The first one thousand air rifles produced by BSA in August, 1905, were identical mechanically to the Lincoln Jeffries 'H' The Lincoln patent model, described in the previous chapter. The serial numbers ran from 1131 to 2129. They were all standard length models supplied with the choice of stock styles of straight hand or pistol hand. Three stock lengths of 13¼″, 13¾″, or 14¼″ were available, the rifle being supplied with a 14¼″ stock as standard unless a shorter length was specified. The BSA Piled Arms Trade Mark was impressed deeply into the left hand face of the stock (see Plate 3). The rearsight was supplied with a standard bar having a wide Vee notch, offered as extra were bars with narrow and shallow Vee notches, half round notches or just a plain bar to be notched as preferred by the user. A variety of foresight types were also offered; the bead type was supplied as standard, but also available was a diamond profile, barleycorn and fine point for use with an American style Buckhorn rearsight bar.

This new BSA product was called simply "The BSA Air Rifle (Lincoln Jeffries' Patent)" and this legend was impressed into the top surface of the cylinder over the statement "Made by the Birmingham Small Arms Co. Ltd."

Whereas Lincoln Jeffries had to rely on direct sales to the public, BSA sold only to the Trade and they already had distributors in most large towns throughout the Kingdom as well as agents or representatives in all major countries of the world. BSA also, of course, had contacts with Government purchasing departments through their War Office contracts in supplying military weapons. Rifles from their first batch were sent to Australia, New Zealand, where an example was awarded a Gold Medal at the Christchurch Exhibition of 1906, Ireland and most amazingly, to India where the rifles proved ideal in rodent control in military corn stores.

The Company also had entirely new outlets for the air rifle in the form of the network of bicycle dealers of which there was one in every small town and village, most of which were serviced by a railway station in the very comprehensive rail system of Edwardian Britain. Sales, therefore, were not restricted to Gun and Firearms dealers but were also made to Sports Shops, Ironmongers, General Stores and Cycle Dealers. Anyone writing to BSA for details of the new air rifle could be given the name of a local stockist or if one was not available, private individuals would be supplied by post or rail direct. The retail profit in the transaction was credited to the account of the nearest BSA dealer, which generous action, of course, encouraged him to stock the new air rifle.

The first rifles left the Small Heath factory on 7th September, 1905 and by the end of January, 1906, the majority of the batch of rifles had left for their various destinations at home and to the far flung corners of the Empire.

Although every effort was made to despatch rifles almost by return against orders received, this unusual haste was to prove time consuming and expensive for the Company in the long run. Fifty-four of the first despatch were returned under complaint within one week of despatch. Most were rectified and returned within the week, some even on the same day. One serious problem was the poor fit of the breech plug in the breech, resulting in misalignment of the pellet chamber with the bore. This was caused by poor hand fitting. The rifle assemblers at BSA were used to working on military arms, all the parts for which were fully interchangeable and military rifle assembly required only the minimum of hand fitting work. This problem did not arise at the Lincoln Jeffries factory as the employees there were well used to skilled hand work, being used to working on high quality English shotguns. The problem was soon corrected at BSA by instigating more carefully supervised hand lapping of the breech plugs during assembly.

Another serious problem was the failure of users to fully understand the new and, to them, quite complicated procedure of cocking and loading the rifle. If the loading pellet chamber of the breech plug was charged with a pellet and the lever returned to the closed position **before** cocking the rifle, the pellet would be sucked back through the transfer port into the chamber. On firing the now empty rifle, the piston would slam forwards, the pellet becoming embedded into the soft leather piston washer, causing damage to its sealing properties. Damage was also caused by the use of conventional straight sided lead airgun slugs instead of waisted diablo type pellets. The slugs were often cheaply made, irregular in size and often too light to effect a satisfactory seal in the barrel in which they would become lodged. Correctly shaped and sized Diablo air rifle pellets were marketed by BSA for use in their rifles. These were manufactured by a local presswork company, Cox & Son, 137A Guildford Street, Lozells, Birmingham; another brand of pellet was recommended soon afterwards.

In November, 1905, the BSA Company issued a descriptive pamphlet giving particulars of the various characteristics of the design of their new air rifle. Being aware of the pellet problem already mentioned, the Company had undertaken various extensive tests with all brands of pellets on the market. They recommended the "Witton" pellet, made by Kynochs of Birmingham, as being the most suitable for accurate results in their air rifles. The "Witton" was the forerunner of the Eley Wasp and BSA Plyarm pellet of today. It was of waisted shape having a skirt diameter of .006" greater than that of the head ensuring concentric positioning in the bore with excellent sealing properties.

In spite of these initial setbacks, the BSA air rifle was very well received and if the returned rifles are considered as a percentage of the total produced, a failure figure of just over 5½% is exceptionally small, even by today's standards with highly automated and computerised inspection systems.

The BSA Company promoted their new rifle whenever possible, one of their most successful ventures being at the Stanley Cycle Show of 1905, held at Islington in London.

At this event BSA installed a well equipped miniature air rifle range with the object of introducing the new air rifle to the visiting public. It was reported in the Trade Press that great interest was shown and all eleven air rifles were in constant demand throughout the duration of the event. It is obvious that a small quantity of rifles were specially prepared from the first batch for use at such promotions.

Sample rifles were sent by the BSA London Office, situated at 6 Great Winchester Street, to the editors of both Trade Monthly Magazines, *Arms and Explosives* and *The Sporting Goods Review and the Gunmaker*. The latter magazine carried a full page editorial with photographs of the BSA Air Rifle in its November 1905 issue. These two publications would have been read by all of the Gun Trade and also by Sports Goods and Cycle dealers. Air rifle competitions using the new BSA Air Rifle were sponsored by the Company in most major towns and at such an event at the Agricultural Hall in London, on 24th November, 1905, a local marksman, Mr. A. E. Hall, shot a remarkable score of seven bulls with seven shots at a range of 10 yards.

BSA could not have launched their new product at a better, more receptive time. Air gun clubs were being started almost daily. During the previous June, a National Air Gun Shoot was held at the Curzon Hall, Birmingham, which attracted entries from 1,000 Airgun Clubs from the Midlands alone. A sample rifle was also sent for demonstration to the National Air Rifle Association Armoury in Birmingham. Old established and respected Gunmakers were now stocking the new BSA Air Rifle. One of the first was Mr. Charles Lancaster of London, who included the BSA Air Rifle in his catalogue, which the journal, *Arms and Explosives,* considered "showed a broadminded tolerance to new developments which are a valuable asset to the Gunmaker who keeps a close watch on the buying and selling aspect of his business".

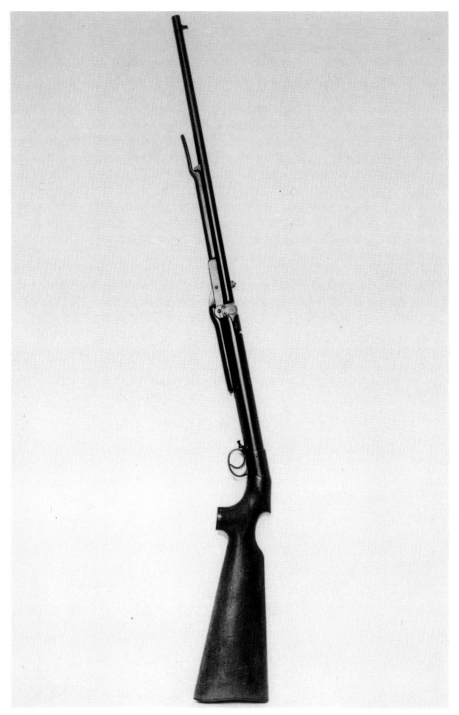
PLATE 15 *(G. Kerry)*
The BSA Air Rifle, Improved Model with improved Breech Plug Fastening Plate.

B.S.A. Military Air-Rifle

(See Plates in body of this Work).

PRICE 80/- EACH.

The weight, balance, and sights are the same as those of the ·303 Long Lee-Enfield Service Rifle.

The Military Air Rifle possesses the same general "feel" as the Service Rifle, and is used in many Drill Halls for instructing recruits in the art of shooting. It is also found invaluable by efficient marksmen as a means of maintaining their skill during the winter months at a minimum of expense.

Comparing the Air Rifle with other methods of giving miniature range practice, its purchase may be recommended as a sound commercial speculation, in that the original cost is covered by the saving effected in the first 7000 rounds used. That is to say, a B.S.A. Military Air Rifle and 7000 rounds of ammunition cost about the same sum of money as 7000 rounds of ordinary ·22 ammunition alone, or 3000 rounds of Morris Tube ammunition.

The rifle is used by many regiments, including
    The Royal Horse Guards.
    The 1st V.B. Royal Warwickshire Regt.
    The Central London Rangers.

Sole Manufacturers . .

THE BIRMINGHAM SMALL ARMS CO., LTD.,

BIRMINGHAM.

1907

PLATE 16 *(G. Kerry)*
An advertisement for the First Pattern BSA Military Air Rifle from the BSA booklet of 1907, and 'The Complete Air Gunner', by R. B. Townsend, M.A.

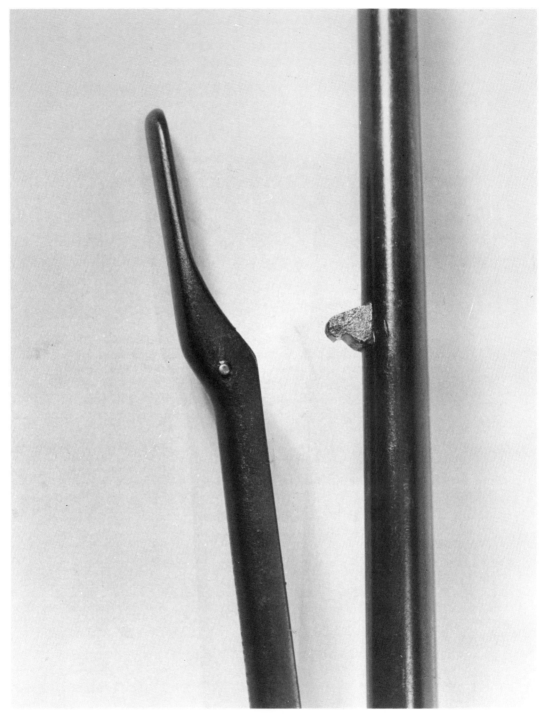

PLATE 17 *(G. Kerry)*
Details of Second Pattern Cocking Lever Catch with strengthening fillets.

Chapter 5

WITH THE BSA Air Rifle being accepted by the public so quickly and so completely, it was ironic that during the same period, sales of Mr. Lincoln Jeffries' Lincoln air rifle were making very slow and heavy progress. It appeared that every marketing method which he instigated, such as sponsorship, demonstrations and exhibitions, if successful, was immediately adopted by BSA who, with their greater expertise, and of course, larger advertising purse, turned Lincoln Jeffries' efforts to their own advantage.

To be fair, however, to BSA, they were a large, publicly owned concern, striving not only to make a profit, but more importantly, for survival. Examining the rather unbusinesslike agreement between the two companies, eighty years later, it is now so obvious that only the stronger, and more financially secure, of the two parties could have succeeded. Fortunately for air rifle design and development, Mr. Lincoln Jeffries did not give up the fight easily and it can be attributed to this great urge of his to succeed and to be fully recognised as the brilliant inventor that he was, which resulted in several more improvements to his original design and indeed, as we shall see, to quite revolutionary new ideas in air rifle manufacture.

The most obvious factor controlling the public acceptance of the Lincoln Air Rifle was that, except for superficial markings, it was identical to the now very well known BSA Air Rifle. In a matter of under six months the invention initially hailed as the Lincoln, a brainchild of Mr. Lincoln Jeffries, was being referred to as a BSA idea and development. At the time that the manufacturing terms were being discussed, it was agreed between the two parties that there should be no retail differential between the two models. In fact, the BSA model was only sold to the trade under the strict condition that retail prices would be maintained. Both models retailed at 50/- (£2.50) for the Pistol Hand version, or as referred to by Mr. Lincoln Jeffries, Registered Stock, and 45/- (£2.25) for the rifle with straight hand stock.

The second batch of Lincoln rifles to be manufactured by BSA were allocated the serial numbers 2130 to 2729. Already the quantity had been decreased by 400 rifles from the first batch supplied. BSA would not have objected too much to this reduction as production of their own model was at that time only just matching demand. It took almost six months for the Lincoln Jeffries factory to take delivery of the first 500 rifles from this second allocation. After rifle number 2626 had been delivered, BSA were requested to hold up delivery on any more Lincoln rifles as a very important and interesting new improvement was in the pipeline, which would certainly affect future demand for this slow moving model, marketed under the Lincoln Jeffries name of the LINCOLN AIR RIFLE.

The new version of the Lincoln had, in fact, already been announced through the Trade Journals way back in November, 1905. Although heralded as a completely new model, the rifle was in fact a shorter and lighter weight version of the ordinary Lincoln rifle, designed for use by Ladies.

At a period in British and Colonial history when the Women's Suffrage Movement was gaining in popularity, only such an inventive genius as Mr. Lincoln Jeffries, would have thought of using woman's emancipation to rejuvenate his ailing sales. He called the new model ''The Ladies Pattern''. It was four inches shorter and one pound three ounces lighter than the Lincoln Ordinary pattern. The cylinder was marked 'L The Lincoln Air Rifle Patent' manufactured by the BSA Co. Ltd., Birmingham (see Plate 10).

A sample ''Ladies Pattern'' rifle was sent for appraisal to the editor of *Arms and Explosives Journal,* who pronounced the new rifle . . . ''. . . one of the neatest and handiest air guns we have ever handled''.

BSA were commissioned by Mr. Lincoln Jeffries to manufacture the new Ladies Pattern rifle entirely at their works and to deliver completed, packed rifles to Steelhouse Lane. The first ten rifles were delivered on 2nd July, 1906, with a further two dozen following on 4th August. In all, 70 rifles were made by BSA to this pattern, the remaining 30 rifles from the batch of 600 were the last ones to be partly assembled by BSA to be finished by Lincoln Jeffries. Hereonafter, all Lincoln Air Rifles were made and finished entirely at the BSA factory, or were supplied without breech plugs to be fitted with the several patented designs of breech plug fittings which Mr. Lincoln Jeffries developed in an endeavour to provide a more air tight fitment and supply a distinctly different feature to his air rifle. The Steelhouse Lane factory of Lincoln Jeffries was now used mainly for warehousing and distribution of Lincoln pattern air rifles.

The Ladies Pattern was assembled from standard BSA components with the minimum of modification. The barrel length was reduced from 19¼" to 17". The cylinder length was reduced from 8½" to 7⅛". The lengths of the hand lever and cocking link were reduced from 12" to 9¼" and from 7" to 6" respectively. A shorter piston and piston rod was required for the reduced cylinder and the mainspring was reduced from 40 to 30¾ coils. BSA already offered short 13¼" length straight hand stocks and these components were fitted to all but one of the 68 new model rifles. The sights, breech plug assembly and trigger block and trigger were all standard parts.

The one Lincoln rifle, serial number 2679, not fitted with a straight hand stock was in fact taken into stock by BSA themselves on 6th September, 1906. Obviously, their intention was to carry out tests with this new rifle with a possible view, if it proved to be accepted by lady shooters, of producing a similar rifle under the BSA banner. It was fitted with a cut down BSA Pistol Hand stock 13¼" long and was retained for future investigative work.

Between January and August, 1906, BSA had assembled and despatched from Small Heath, 2,100 of their BSA Air Rifles. Such was the demand now for the new target rifle due in no small way to the outstanding success of ''BSA Air Rifle'' users in competitive shooting, that rifles were being despatched as quickly as they could be made. In March, 1906, it was reported that Mr. James T. Clayton of Macclesfield and District

Air Rifle Association, at a shoot at Congleton in Cheshire, won First Prize with 16 consecutive bulls eyes. In April, Mr. Clayton went on to win a shield in an All England Competition. He, of course, was shooting a BSA Air Rifle. In the early part of the year, despatches of lots of 7, 8, 11 or a dozen rifles, were common place but by early summer, lots of 20 or 30 rifles were being ordered by the Trade. The serial numbers of this batch ran from 2730 to 4829.

Mainly to help production, but also to improve the rifle generally, BSA were constantly reviewing the Lincoln Jeffries design and one of the first improvements made was to the trigger guard.

The original Lincoln Jeffries trigger guard with its long flat tang, was awkward and time consuming to fit. Two types had also to be kept in stock for straight and pistol hand stocks. Being of cast iron construction, they were also very easily broken in storage and assembly. The BSA designers came up with a new universal trigger guard suitable for both forms of stock shape. The long rang was removed and a small ⅛″ diameter pip, or peg, was formed on the rear of the guard which fitted into a hole drilled in the back of the trigger block behind the trigger recess (see Plate 11). It was a simple matter to modify existing stocks of trigger blocks and both types of trigger guards and trigger blocks were used in assembly during the production of this batch of rifles, collectors will find combinations of all types between these serial numbers. The first recorded modified trigger guard was fitted to BSA Air Rifle No. 3870.

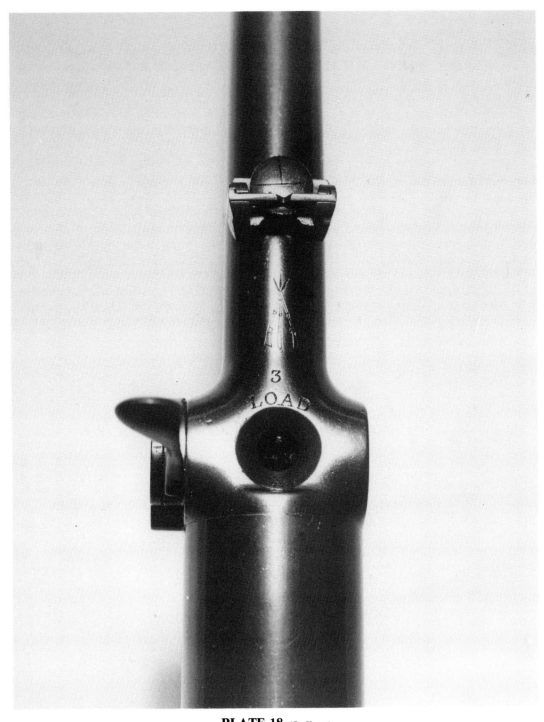

PLATE 18 *(G. Kerry)*
No. 3 (.250″) Improved Model 'D' with No. 10 Rearsight.

PLATE 19 *(G. Kerry)*

An advertisement from 'The Scout' magazine of 1908. By this date almost 20,000 Air Rifles had been produced, not 200,000 as suggested. This is the first known advertisement for the No. 3 (.250″) Calibre Rifle.

PLATE 20 *(G. Kerry)*
Details of Model 12 Aperture Rearsight.

Chapter 6

THE THIRD batch of Lincoln Air Rifles to be made at BSA comprised 1,000 rifles, 100 of which were finished in the new Ladies Pattern. The serial numbers of the batch ran from 4830 to 5829. They were sent out of the BSA factory in quite large consignments of up to 80 rifles; the average despatch being of 50 units. This batch proved to have quite a combination of modifications; some of the rifles were fitted with the last of the stock of long tang cast trigger guards but where convenient, the new small peg fitting BSA type of guard was used. Some rifles, for example, number 5187, had the latest type of BSA trigger block drilled to accept the new type of trigger guard, but was fitted with a long tang early specimen of trigger guard, possibly to use up stocks of old guards.

The most unusual feature regarding this batch was the different types of breech plug fitting used. Mr. Lincoln Jeffries had perfected a new method of securing the breech plug which he considered to be more efficient than the previously used BSA method of using the large headed screw and keeper screw. The new Lincoln Jeffries design did away with these two components and instead exposed the projecting right hand portion of the plug with its square shoulder and threaded hole. On to this was fitted a large bearing washer retained by a large knurled steel finger nut under which was a compensating spring. The intention was that wear on the plug would be taken up by the spring and by the action of tightening the knurled nut (see Plate 12). This system was used for many of the Lincoln rifles but was not as efficient a system of fastening as the BSA Improved system to be detailed later. With the Lincoln Jeffries adjustable system, when any wear did occur, the result of tightening the fastening nut was to pull the pellet hole out of line with the bore (see Plate 63 and 64).

For unknown reasons, not all of the rifles in this batch had this unusual breech plug fitting; some of the later manufacture rifles reverted to the original BSA method used on previous production rifles. Both methods of plug fixing used the same diameter of breech plug and required the use of a seating pin or pellet pusher to enable the pellet to be correctly seated in the breech plug chamber.

Despatch of this 1,000 Lincoln Air Rifles from the BSA factory started in late January, 1906 and was completed by mid September of that year. During the year 1906, there were five applications for breech plug securing methods, one from BSA and four from Lincoln Jeffries. BSA's application was the first applied for. A design by Lincoln Jeffries in which the breech plug operating lever worked in a slot milled in the fixed breech of the rifle was applied for only a few weeks later. The similarity of design caused a patent wrangle which accounts for the long delay in granting the BSA 8246/06 patent. As the patent was granted to BSA, they obviously put forward a better claim. Lincoln Jeffries design was accepted on 10th January, 1907 and given patent number 11588-06. This was, however, later amended by the Patent Office and reprinted on 20th June, 1907. It is reasonable to assume that during late 1906, early 1907, at least five different breech plug retaining systems were used on air rifles manufactured under Lincoln Jeffries Trade Mark, although to date, examples of all five have not been positively identified.

The third batch of BSA air rifles to be produced were 2,000 in number and were numbered 5830 to 7829. They were still the standard, or ordinary, pattern retaining the same distinctive BSA markings on the air cylinder, i.e.

The BSA Air Rifle (Lincoln Jeffries' patent)

Made by the Birmingham Small Arms Company Ltd.

However, included in this batch was one rifle which was the result of BSA's evaluation of the Lincoln Jeffries Ladies Pattern Rifle No. 2679, retained by them for examination in September, 1906. This rifle, No. 6112, was made to the same Ladies Pattern specification with a 13¼ straight hand stock and it was despatched on 9th January, 1907. Despatch of the remainder of this batch started in June, 1906 and was completed by the end of October of that year.

In November, 1906, a patent was granted to BSA in the names of A. H. M. Driver and Mr. G. Norman for an improved system of fastening the breech plug in the breech block. The plug was made shorter and fatter than previously and the hole to accommodate it in the breech block was not drilled completely through; it was in fact blind on the right hand side. The plug was retained from the left hand side by means of a keyhole shaped plate fastened to the breech block with two screws (see Plate 13). The lever end of the plug had a recess in its centre into which fitted a protruding peg on the inside

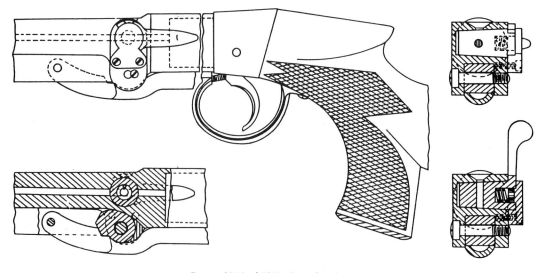

Patent 8246 of 1906. Part drawing.

of the fixing plate. Under this peg was a coil spring to exert pressure on the plug and make its positioning more positive than had previously been possible (see Plate 14). The hole, or pellet chamber, in the plug was enlarged and tapered so that a pellet could now be dropped in by hand doing away with the necessity of the pellet seating pin. This design was granted patent number 8246/06 and accepted on 22nd November, 1906.

In the last quarter of 1906, BSA produced and delivered to Lincoln Jeffries, a fourth batch of 1,000 Lincoln air rifles. These were allocated the serial numbers 7830 to 8829. Most of these rifles had the new BSA patent loading tap keyhole shaped, retaining plate. However, at that time, Mr. Lincoln Jeffries had been working on more improvements to loading tap fixtures and in September, 1906, had designed an unusual method of loading plug retention by means of a spring arm or limb which pivoted in the threaded hole which usually accommodated the cocking lever axis screw keeper screw. A patent for this design was applied for through Mr. Lincoln Jeffries patent agent, G. F. Urry, who was also a valued employee at the Steelhouse Lane factory and was eventually granted in 1907 under patent number 20744/06. This design is known as the Lincoln Jeffries Quick Release Breech Plug Catch, and was fitted to Lincoln Air Rifles as early as September, 1906. The design was not, however, announced to the Trade until May of the following year. The earliest known rifle fitted with this new patent fastening is No. 8218, despatched on 20.10.06. Probably no more than 50 rifles were fitted with this type of breech plug fixing.

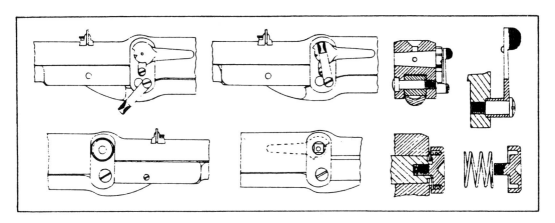

Patent 20744 of 1906. Part drawing. Lincoln Jeffries Quick Release Breech Plug Catch.

The fourth batch of BSA air rifles was produced between October, 1906 and December, 1906. They numbered 1400 units and were serial numbered from 8830 through 10229.

All these rifles had the new form of patented breech plug retaining plate with enlarged pellet chamber in the breech plug itself. These rifles were all of the BSA Improved Pattern. As the new breech plug patent had not been granted when the first batch of retaining plates was manufactured, the plates were marked P.Pat. (see Plate 13). Over 2,000 of these plates were so marked and were still being assembled on rifles many months after the patent was granted a registered number and accepted. The reference to the original Lincoln Jeffries Patent was dropped and the air rifles were now marked on the top of the cylinder with a new, more possessive logo:

"The BSA Air Rifle".

The Birmingham Small Arms Co. Ltd.,

Sole Manufacturers.

The engraving was larger than previous markings and much bolder and more deeply impressed into the steel of the cylinder.

BSA had already decided to market their air rifle as "The Improved BSA Air Rifle" and an advertisement to this effect was published in the January edition of *The Sporting Goods Review and The Gunmaker*. It was advertised as being made completely in the BSA factory with all parts fully interchangeable. The Trade notes in the same edition of the magazine noted that orders were pouring in for the new BSA Improved Air Rifle (see Plate 15).

It is interesting to note that in this particular batch of rifles, BSA produced ten rifles which they called their "Light Pattern Models". These were identical in all respects, with the exception of the improved breech plug retaining plate, to the Lincoln Ladies Pattern rifles produced for Lincoln Jeffries. The Sales Department of BSA had obviously been watching with interest the reception of the Ladies version of the Lincoln and having confirmed its acceptance by the public, were now intending to add this new model to their own range. By advertising a new "Improved Model BSA Air Rifle", BSA were further disassociating themselves from the Lincoln Jeffries association. In the BSA Publication of August, 1907, under the title "The Improved BSA Air Rifle", no reference at all was made to any Lincoln Jeffries designs or developments.

The improvements on the previous designs were claimed as:
1. The barrel and breech are in one piece.
2. There are no joints, as in break barrel models, to get loose.
3. The use of a separate cocking lever, prevents damage to the barrel.
4. The accurately fitting breech plug allows easy loading whilst maintaining an airtight seal.
5. The improved design of backsight allows for the smallest changes of elevation whilst allowing for the use of interchangeable sight bars.
6. The barrel is bored and rifled with the same precision as a Service Rifle Barrel, but to a specification developed specially for airgun pellets.
7. Worn mainsprings may be replaced easily without the use of special tools.

It will be noticed that all of these features, with the exception of the loading plug, are not in fact new but were features of the original Lincoln Jeffries design.

Elsewhere in the leaflet, actual improvments made by BSA are detailed. These are all attributed to the new design of breech plug and are listed as follows:

1. The pellet seating pin is no longer required.
2. The rifle can be loaded directly by hand due to the enlarged pellet hole.
3. There are larger wearing surfaces and fewer parts to get out of order.

4. There is no longer need to adjust the breech plug for wear which is taken up automatically.
5. The breech plug can be easily removed to enable the bore to be examined.

It was emphasised that every BSA Air Rifle has that title inscribed on the cylinder and the Company's trade mark of three piled rifles is impressed in the stock. Almost every page of the leaflet carried the sentence "Manufactured only by the Birmingham Small Arms Company Limited". Here again, we see an attempt being made to identify the BSA Air Rifle as being 100% a BSA innovation.

The first official reference to the BSA Light Pattern Air rifle is made in the new publication. It is described as being specially suitable for Ladies and Youths and is claimed to have already been selected for use by junior members of Schools, Lads' Brigades etc. This claim is substantiated by the reproduction of several letters from Headmasters etc. praising the Light Pattern model. The rifle was advertised with the choice of straight or pistolhand stock at the same price as the standard, ordinary pattern air rifle.

The descriptive leaflet contained one very unusual feature in that in the publication is printed an exploded diagram of the air rifle with nomenclature of parts. This rifle is depicted with a trigger spring, adjusting screw and trigger guard of a type not produced commercially by BSA.

It can only be suspected that a design drawing was used for illustration purposes to save time and expense in having a special accurate diagram produced for this publication depicting an actual production rifle. The list of parts also includes the now obsolete large headed loading tap retaining screw and keeper screw and omits the keyhole shaped breech plug retaining plate shown on the diagram!

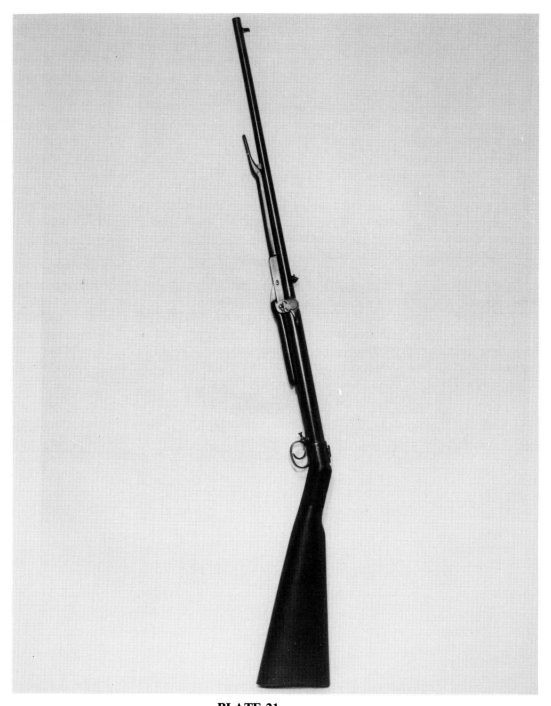

PLATE 21 *(G. Kerry)*
.177 Improved Model 'D' Standard Pattern with No. 12 Aperture Sight fitted into the top of
the Trigger Block.

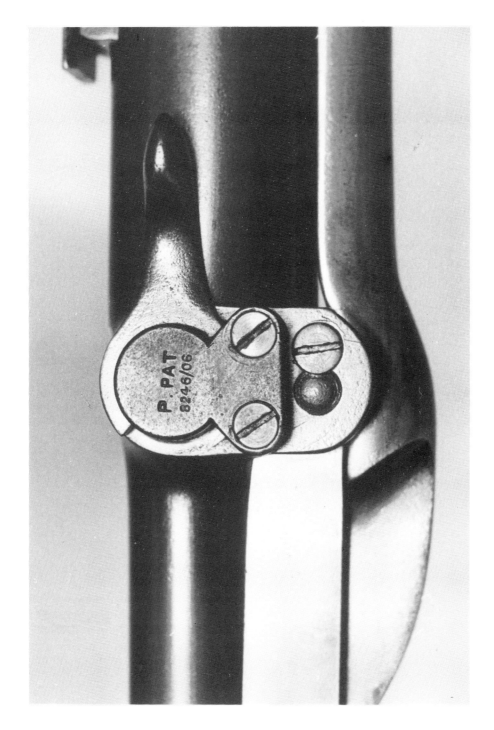

PLATE 22 *(G. Kerry)*
Improved Breech Plug and Retaining Plate with Indexing Plunger and Spring—Early Pattern.

PLATE 23 *(G. Kerry)*
Fixing Screw in cylinder of 'H Lincoln Air Rifle' seventh batch.
This screw was also fitted to some BSA Improved Model 'D' Rifles.

Chapter 7

IN A TRADE Journal of March, 1907, mention was made of the still unprecedented increase in air rifle shooting generally and it was remarked that the sport promised to be all the year round amusement. It also noted that the BSA Air Rifle was selling very well and owing to the Company's world wide trade, a much larger variety of sizes is having to be produced.

This statement was obviously the result of a Company Press Release to prepare the Trade for various new BSA models.

A BSA Military Pattern Air Rifle was launched at the 1907 Bisley Meeting where it caused great interest and was publicised as a new BSA Model designed specially for use by Schools, Cadet Forces, Volunteer Brigades and Territorial Forces. The trade journal, *Arms and Explosives,* of August, 1907, felt it necessasry, however, to point out to its readers that the BSA Military Air Rifle which had caused such a stir at Bisley, was not in fact a BSA conception at all and the Editor took great pains to give credit for its development to the Westley Richards Company. This did not, however, deter BSA from taking a full page advertisement for their Military Pattern Air Rifle in the new handbook of air gun shooting entitled "The Complete Air Gunner", written by R. B. Townsend M.A., published in August of that year (see Plate 16). More will be written of the BSA Air Rifle Military Patterns in a later chapter.

In October, 1906, Lincoln Jeffries & Company Limited, was registered as a Limited Company with a capital of 1,000 of £1.00 shares in order to acquire the business of George Lincoln Jeffries. All 'H The Lincoln' Air Rifles being produced by BSA were now marked with a new bolder cylinder inscription which read "H The Lincoln Air Rifle Patent 1904/5". The fifth batch of Lincolns was allocated the serial numbers 10230 to 11229. Despatch from BSA started in November, 1906 and all but 100 rifles were despatched by the end of August, 1907. 98 rifles, serial number 10410 up to 10507 were, for an unspecified reason, not despatched to Lincoln Jeffries until August and September, 1908, one year later. The two remaining rifles in this batch were numbers 10849 and 11135.

By now all BSA rifles were being assembled with the new breech plug system and all were of the Improved Model. Stocks of components for the earlier type of breech plug style with large screw and keeper fixtures were being used up for the production of Lincoln air rifles, the contract for which had still quite a long way to run.

All the Lincoln rifles despatched in 1906-7, had either the breech plug fitted with the spring compensated knurled nut already described, or the now obsolete first pattern BSA type of breech plug retained by the large screw and keeper. Standard and Ladies Patterns were included in this batch (see Plate 66).

There has been no opportunity to examine any of the 100 rifles despatched in 1908 so it is difficult to offer an explanation for the segregation and late despatch of these rifles. It is possible that they were all produced in No. 3 (.250″) calibre as at that period (late 1908), rifles of similar bore were being made by BSA under their own brand name. The reason for the twelve months delay in despatch can be attributed to the practice adopted by BSA in the allocation of serial numbers. Numbers already allocated to Lincoln Jeffries would be reserved in the ledgers until such time as weapons could be produced against those particular numbers.

The fifth batch of rifles produced under the BSA name followed on directly from the 4th batch. 2,000 serial numbers were allocated from 11230 up to 13229. In this batch, were the long production runs of the new Light Pattern rifles. A total of 170 Light Pattern rifles was assembled. Obviously, from the records, manufacture was to special order as both straight hand and pistol hand style stocks were supplied, of all three lengths. These small rifles were not despatched in any particular sequence but from the despatch dates they all appeared to be part of quite large orders, the bulk of which were for ordinary pattern rifles. The despatch details suggest that regular buyers of the BSA Air Rifle were taking one or two of the new Light Patterns into stock, probably on the advice of BSA salesmen, to see how they would be received by the public. Of the 170 rifles made, the quantity of straight or pistol hand stocks is almost equal so it is possible that retailers took with their usual order one of each stock style of Light Pattern rifles.

This batch of rifles was one of the last to be made by BSA with the cylinder inscription

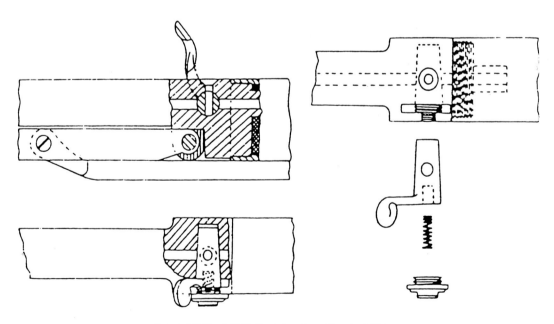

Patent 11588 of 1906. Part drawing. Lincoln Jeffries.

"The BSA Air Rifle". The entire batch was despatched between 1st December, 1906 and the end of August, 1907.

Between June, 1908 and September, 1908, the last but one batch of Lincoln air rifles was sent to Steelhouse Lane. Serial numbers ran from 13230 through to 14229. In this batch were a variety of breech plug fitments. Most had the knurled nut and compensating spring fitting. One known rifle, serial number 13827, from this batch had an experimental style of breech plug with the operating lever working in a milled slot in the breech. This design was patented by Lincoln Jeffries and allocated number 11588/06 and granted to them immediately after patent 8246/06 was granted to BSA.

Another interesting rifle from this batch is numbered 13992. This is fitted with a BSA style breech plug retained by the patented plate but is one of the first rifles known to have the cocking link axis screw locked by means of a keeper screw. One annoying complaint with all previous production BSA and Lincoln air rifles was the tendency of the cocking link axis screw to work loose during usage of the rifle. Whether BSA or Lincoln Jeffries were the first company to fit a locking keeper screw to this component, is a matter of conjecture. BSA took advantage of this modification to advertise at a later date that all axis screws on their Improved Rifle were locked with keeper screws.

PLATE 24 *(G. Kerry)*
.22″ Improved Model 'D' 45½″ long with No. 19 Folding Rearsight.

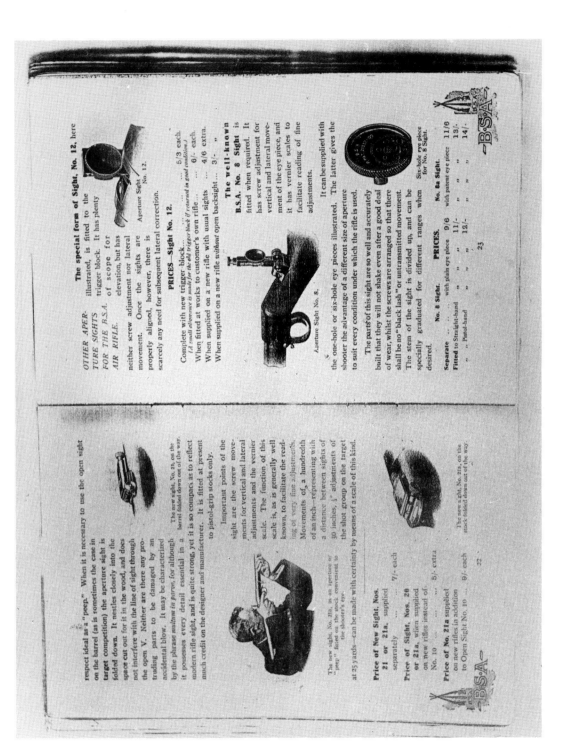

OTHER APER-
TURE SIGHTS
FOR THE B.S.A.
AIR RIFLE.

The special form of Sight, No. 12, here illustrated, is fitted to the trigger block. It has plenty of scope for elevation, but has neither screw adjustment nor lateral movement. Once the sights are properly aligned, however, there is scarcely any need for subsequent lateral correction.

Aperture Sight No. 12.

PRICES—Sight No. 12.

Complete with new trigger block...   5/3 each.
(A small allowance is made for the old trigger block if returned in good condition.)
When fitted at works to customer's own rifle...   6/- each.
When supplied on a new rifle with usual sights ... 4/6 extra.
When supplied on a new rifle without open backsight... 3/- ...

The well-known B.S.A. No. 8 Sight is fitted when required. It has screw adjustment for vertical and lateral movement of the eye piece, and it has vernier scales to facilitate reading of fine adjustments.

Aperture Sight No. 8.

It can be supplied with the one-hole or six-hole eye pieces illustrated. The latter gives the shooter the advantage of a different size of aperture to suit every condition under which the rifle is used.

The parts of this sight are so well and accurately built that they will not shake even after a good deal of wear, whilst the screws are arranged so that there shall be no "black lash" or untransmitted movement. The stem of the sight is divided up, and can be specially graduated for different ranges when desired.

PRICES.

	No. 8 Sight.	No. 8a Sight. Six-hole eye piece for No. 8 Sight.
	with plain eye piece	with patent eye piece
Separate ...	9/6	11/6
Fitted to Straight-hand " "	11/-	13/-
" Pistol-hand " "	12/-	14/-

23

respect ideal as a "peep." When it is necessary to use the open sight on the barrel (as is sometimes the case in target competition) the aperture sight is folded down. It nestles closely into the space cut out for it in the wood, and does not interfere with the line of sight through the open V. Neither are there any protruding parts to be damaged by an accidental blow. It may be characterized by the phrase multum in parvo, for although it possesses every detail essential in a modern rifle sight, and is quite strong, yet it is so compact as to reflect much credit on the designer and manufacturer.

The new sight, No. 21, as an aperture or "peep" fitted on the stock, convenient to the shooter's eye.

The new sight, No. 21, on the barrel folded down out of the way.

Important points of the sight are the screw movements for vertical and lateral adjustments and the vernier scale. The function of this scale is, as is generally well known, to facilitate the reading of very fine adjustments. Movements of a hundredth of an inch—representing with a distance between sights of 30 inches, ⅓" adjustments of the shot group on the target at 25 yards—can be made with certainty by means of a scale of this kind.

Price of New Sight, Nos. 21 or 21a, supplied separately   ...   7/- each

Price of Sight, Nos. 20 or 21a, when supplied on new rifles instead of No. 10   ...   5/- extra

Price of No. 21a supplied on new rifles in addition to Open Sight No. 10 ... 9/- each

The new sight, No. 21a, on the stock folded down out of the way.

22

PLATE 25 *(G. Kerry)*
Details of Aperture Sights mentioned in the BSA Booklet of 1911.

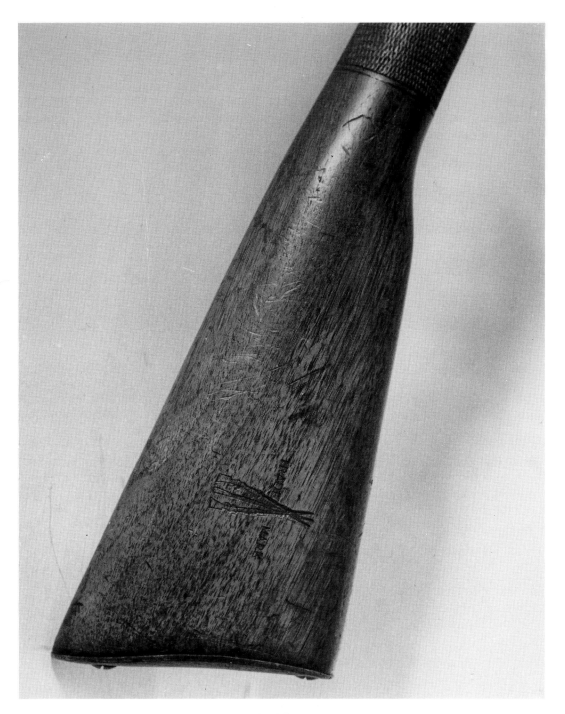

PLATE 26 *(G. Kerry)*
Details of the diminutive 11¼″ long straight hand stock fitted to the first
Junior Pattern Improved Model 'D'.

Chapter 8

BY THE SUMMER of 1907, air rifle shooting as a competitive sport was at its height. Many companies, hitherto unconnected with air rifles, were taking advantage of the vast new market this branch of shooting had generated. The firm of J. Stanton of Wolverhampton, who were famous throughout gunmaking circles for the very high quality of their gun locks and springs, were now making metal targets for air rifle clubs which, they claimed, were so well made that they could be used with BSA and other powerful rifles.

After Mr. Balfour, the Prime Minister, had given Government sanction to air rifle club shooting by stating that "any man who could shoot was a soldier half made", BSA even gave their workers the benefit of the new sport (and of their increased profits from it) by opening an air rifle range at Small Heath, entirely for use by Company workers. This range boasted six targets which could be wound back to the firing point for changing. Bell target shooting at six yards range was beginning to replace even skittles in both town and country pubs and soon bell target leagues were formed similar to darts leagues of modern times.

The May, 1907 trade journals carried an announcement that Mr. Lincoln Jeffries had introduced to his latest rifles a new type of breech plug fastening (see Plate 12). This was in the form of an adjustable thumb screw or knurled nut which could be used to adjust wear on the plug and also enabled the plug to be easily removed so that the bore could be examined. It was stated that this form of fitting could be supplied to all rifles of BSA make and in future would be supplied at no extra cost to all Lincoln Jeffries future production.

This fitting, it should be remembered, was actually supplied to rifles of the third Lincoln Jeffries batch. The late announcement was probably to clarify and justify this different fitting against the BSA Improved Breech Plug design which was being so vigorously advertised by BSA.

Later, however, in October, 1907, Mr. Lincoln Jeffries and Mr. G. F. Urry, were granted Patent 21324/06 to cover yet another form of self-adjusting, quick release breech plug fastening. In this patent, the tapered breech plug was held in place by means of an angled spring loaded wedge bearing on a similarly angled slot machined in the plug body. Spring tension could be controlled by a screw and if required, the plug could be removed by hand by raising a projecting button fastened to the locking wedge. As

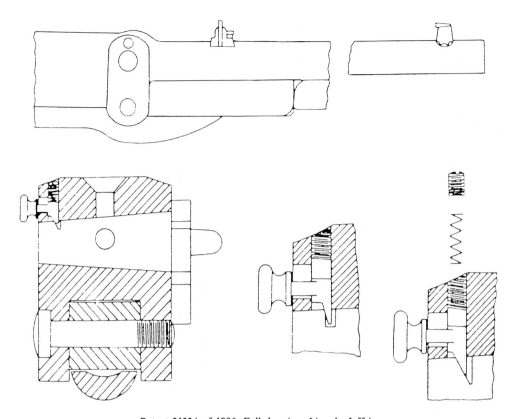

Patent 21324 of 1906. Full drawing. Lincoln Jeffries.

far as is known, no rifles bearing this improved breech plug retaining system were ever put on to the market.

In the spring of 1907, production of the BSA air rifle was at its height. The factory were completing more than 150 rifles of both patterns each day and still finding it hard to meet the many orders coming in, especially from abroad. At the same time sales for the Lincoln air rifle were very poor. No more were finished for Lincoln Jeffries until the spring of 1908 and even then, rifles were only produced under the Lincoln banner to enforce the contract between the two companies and, more importantly, to clear stocks of components peculiar only to the Lincoln models.

The rifles being produced by BSA, under their own name, were the Improved models but they were still engraved on the cylinder with their title "The BSA Air Rifle". The Company had been marketing this model for some time now under the banner of "The Improved Model" yet there was no indication on the rifle itself to differentiate the "Improved Model" from the previous BSA Air Rifle. The Company had had to rely on prospective purchasers either reading their literature detailing the new improvements, or by being advised by the retailer at the point of sale. As previously mentioned, component parts were made in quite large batches and in any major or minor model change, existing stocks of components had to be used up before modified or changed replacement components were issued to the Assembly Department.

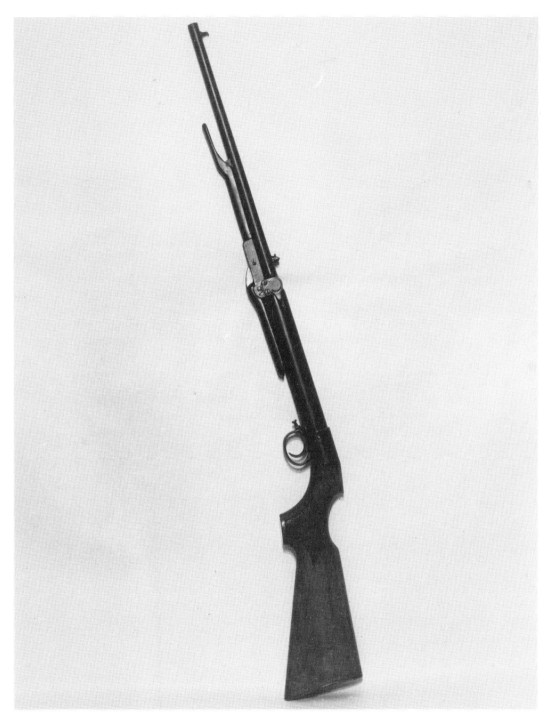

PLATE 27 *(G. Kerry)*
Junior Pattern Air Rifle Improved Model 'D'.

PLATE 28 *(G. Kerry)*
Details of the cover of the comprehensive Air Rifle Booklet issued by BSA in 1911.

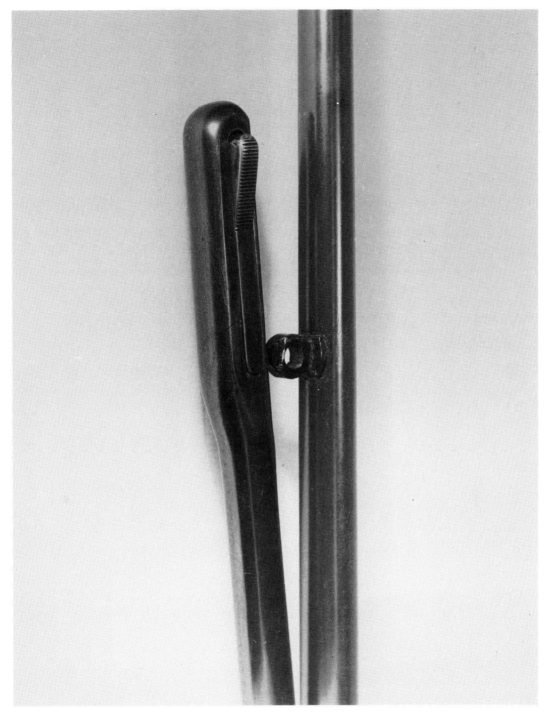

PLATE 29 *(G. Kerry)*
Details of Side Button Cocking Lever Catch. Lincoln Jeffries Patent 25783/10.

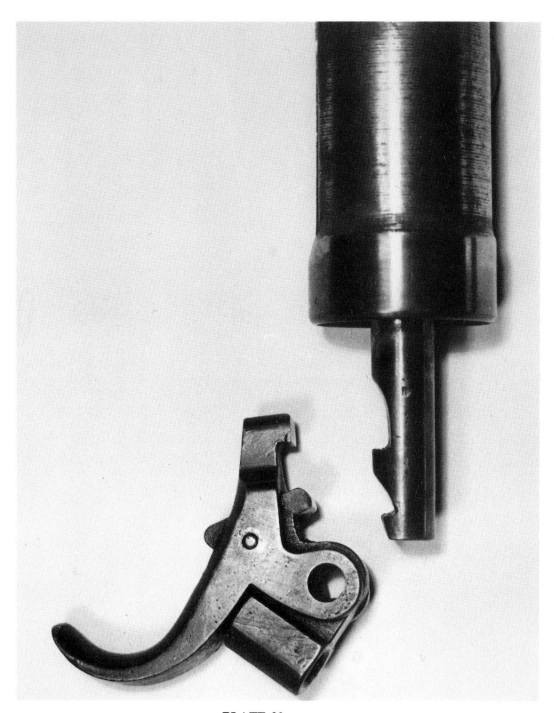

PLATE 30 *(G. Kerry)*
Double Safe Sear showing double bent piston rod and Safety Sear on trigger.
Patent 30338-10. Early 1913.

Chapter 9

TOWARDS THE end of February, 1907, it was decided to make several more minor improvements to the BSA Air Rifle and to alter its title on the cylinder to show that it was the Improved Model. The BSA Air Rifle had been marketed for several months now as the improved model. Dealers had had ample opportunity to dispose of old stocks, as too had wholesalers. Demand for the improved rifles was sufficient for a major change in brand name to be made. It was decided, therefore, to call the slightly improved model "The BSA Air Rifle (Improved Model B)".

During the week 15th to 20th February, it was discovered that in the registers covering serial numbers issued, there were nearly 100 rifles which for one reason or another, had never been completed or had been returned under complaint, replaced and never rectified. These rifles had been overlooked due to the greater than expected sales of new rifles which did not allow time for any rogue weapons to be rectified for resale.

Instructions were issued for these rifles to be located and, if possible, put into a saleable condition and sent out of the factory as soon as possible. Prominent amongst these rogue rifles was No. 1130, the very first number issued to BSA after production of Mr. Lincoln Jeffries first batch of Lincoln rifles. This rifle was actually despatched from the BSA works on 14th March, 1907, one year, six months and one week after its successor, No. 1131 left the factory. Between 22nd February and 14th October, 98 of these rogue rifles were assembled, inspected and despatched from the factory. With a clean slate, as it were, production could now start on the BSA Air Rifle (Improved Model B) the first of which was No. 14230. The first rifles of this new type to leave the factory were Nos. 14253 and 14271, both of which were despatched on the 18th February. Soon after this date, some rifles were assembled using the old cylinders bearing the inscription "The BSA Air Rifle" but these rifles were assembled with all the (Improved Model B) characteristics. Some examples of standard or ordinary pattern rifles in the 15,000 series of serial numbers, were not marked with the improved cylinder inscription.

Light Pattern rifles were still being made but not in any significant number. In the first 1,370 (Improved Model B) rifles produced, only 115 were Light Patterns.

The small improvements to the rifle were only very minor. A keeper screw was fitted to the cocking link axis screw; this modification had already proved successful on the 'H The Lincoln' patent 1904/5 rifle.

A two part piston washer was fitted having an outer cup washer with an inner filler washer, in place of the original one piece flat washer. This two piece washer had better sealing qualities and was fitted by the factory and by retailers to older models whenever washers and springs were later renewed. Finally, the mainspring system was changed from a single spring of 40 coils to a pair of opposingly coiled springs, each of 21 coils of very slightly thinner wire. The double spring reduced breakage by making the tempering easier and as they had opposing coils, the torque was reduced giving longer spring life and smoother performance.

Demand, as always, was good for the new rifle and many were now being supplied to large wholesalers. The Army & Navy Co-operative Society Ltd., in London, were placing large contracts for rifles to be impressed with their own name and address. Overseas distributors were also placing contract orders, one of the largest being W. Hazard of Auckland, New Zealand, who also had his name impressed but tended to spoil the rifles on receipt by modifying the stocks to his own special, quite ugly, design.

With such a large number of rifles now in use throughout the world, under all sorts of extreme conditions, more new improvements were suggested to or recognised by BSA. The first improvement was to the hand or cocking lever. The method of holding the lever against the underside of the barrel was by means of a spring loaded shaped plunger or catch, engaging into a hook shaped block fitted into the underside of the barrel. With use, as the wearing surfaces of the axis area became worn, the lever had a tendency to develop excessive lateral movement, making the snap closure of the hand lever uncertain. This movement was controlled by extending the sides of the hand lever on either side of the spring catch to form stengthening fillets or fences (see Plate 17). Rifles numbered from 17,000 has this form of hand catch but examples will be found of higher serial number rifles with early hand levers fitted whilst old stocks were being used up.

Another improvement was a wider, more substantialy rearsight. Known as the No. 10 sight (see Plate 18), basically it was the same as the original in design but was ¾" instead of ½" wide. The sight blade or bar, was more substantial and the elevating screw was twice the diameter and, therefore, much easier to adjust than the original small sight. This improved sight was introduced around serial number 19000 but both sights were used either side of this serial number to enable stocks of the smaller sight to be used up.

The breech plug fixing plates fitted to all these rifles were still marked P. Pat. in spite of the fact that the patent covering this improvement was granted in November, 1906. BSA were using up marked stocks of fixing plates until the patent number could be marked on new production plates.

One interesting point to note, is that all of the hand or cocking levers on these improved rifles were imprinted down their length with the wording "Lincoln Jeffries Patent 8761/04". Which acknowledged his original patent on which all of BSA production was based (see Plate 32).

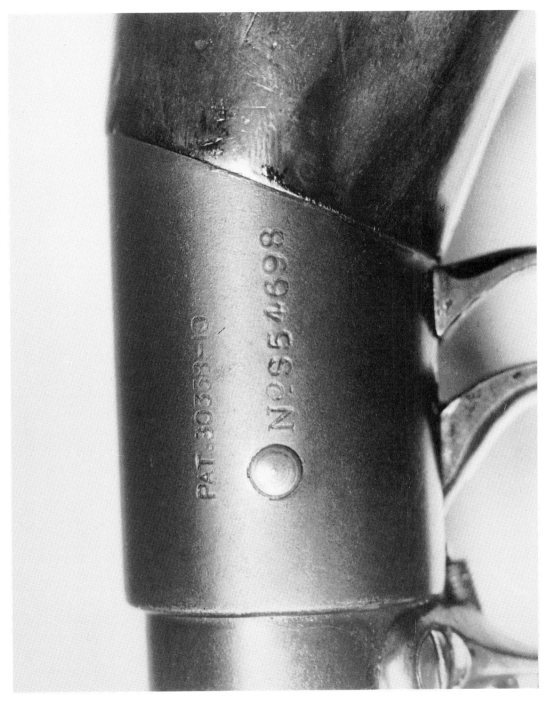

PLATE 31 *(G. Kerry)*
Details of Trigger Block markings on Rifles fitted with Double Safety Sear.
Patent 30338/10.

71

PLATE 32 *(G. Kerry)*
Markings on the Second Pattern Cocking Lever with Strengthening Fillets (left).
Markings on the Side Button Cocking Lever after late 1912 (right).

PLATE 33 *(G. Kerry)*
Late Pattern Junior Air Rifle with Side Button Cocking Lever Catch (right).
Early Pattern Junior Air Rifle with Second Pattern Cocking Lever Catch (left).

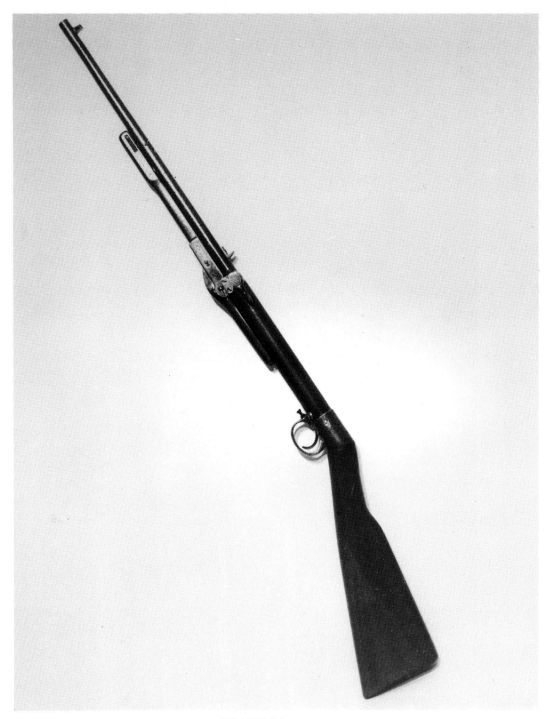

PLATE 34 *(G. Kerry)*
BSA Air Rifle Improved Model 'D' Juvenile Pattern.

Chapter 10

IN MID 1908, the BSA Air Rifle was further improved and resulted in the creation of one of the most widely known and prolific of the pre Great War models; the BSA Air Rifle (Improved Model D). This logo was to last until well into the Great War period and when production ceased in 1918, all three calibres .177, .22 and .250", had been produced with this now famous cylinder inscription and this included Light, Standard or Ordinary, Standard Sporting Pattern (45½") and two models known as the Junior and Juvenile pattern.

The first known "Improved Model D" rifle is Number 19236 which left the factory on 6th May, 1908. As it was of Light pattern with straight hand stock, it is unlikley that it remained in stock for any length of time and it can, therefore, be assumed that the official change-over from "B" to "D" in the descriptive cylinder marking, would have taken place around serial number 19000.

The effect of actually marking a rifle "Improved Model" had a quite remarkable effect on sales. Not only were rifles purchased by persons who had never previously owned a BSA air rifle, but owners of original pattern rifles also purchased the later improved pattern.

Had the BSA designers known that improvements to their rifles would have been progressive, it is certain that they would have called the variously improved models "The Improved Model A, B, C, D, E" etc. However, when any improvements are made to any product; at the time of the improvement, the designers and producers are certain that no other improvements could be made. It is for this reason that no rifles made by BSA were ever marked "Improved Model A". The later production run of "The BSA Air Rifle" were really "Improved Model A" patterns. Likewise, Improved Model B rifles which had modified piston washers and rearsights and strengthening fences on the hand or cocking levers, were technically "Improved Model C" patterns. When further improvements were made in the form of a more substantial foresight with a wider dovetailed base, a larger peg diameter on the rear of the trigger guard, for more positive fixing of this component (see Plate 11) and two new calibres .22" and .250". The new improved model was designated "Improved Model D".

It must be accepted that there was never any definite point in either time or production when any of these changes were made. A stage of production would be decided upon by the Production Manager at which various parts would be modified or replaced.

Obviously, existing parts would not be scrapped but would be used up entirely before the modified components would be issued for assembly. It is for this reason that seemingly obsolete parts are sometimes found on rifles of a much later date, this is particularly evident in the Military pattern models, as will be explained later.

In January of 1908, Mr. Bonehill, the inventor of the Britannia air rifle, introduced a new sporting model called The Belmont. This rifle was made in .250″ calibre which was not a new size of bore as Gem rifles had been sold in this calibre since the turn of the century. The Belmont was, however, the first air gun with a rifled barrel to be produced in this large calibre.

In April of 1908, BSA produced a few models of their "Improved Model D" air rifle in .250″ (No. 3 bore) as a special sporting pattern. These were serial numbered around the 20,000 series and samples were given to travellers and main agents to use to obtain customer reaction and, of course, forward orders. It is still a common practice in the Gun Trade, and in other trades, to try and obtain sufficient forward orders to cover setting up costs before going ahead with full production, of any new product or model.

The new .250″ models were first advertised in a Boy Scout magazine "The Scout" in April, 1908 as a light pattern capable of killing birds at up to 50 yards (see Plate 19). A small quantity were ordered and on the strength of orders received, the new gun went into production. Production started with serial numbers of 21,000 and first despatches began in May, 1908.

In June, 1908, BSA were advertising the new Sporting Pattern BSA air rifle as "Just introduced" and "In Great Demand". The rifle was illustrated and advertised as fitted with aperture back sight. This sight was the No. 12 model which was fitted into a specially milled recess in the top of the trigger block (see Plates 20 and 21).

The very first production rifles were made the same length as the standard or ordinary pattern rifle at 43¼″. Again these early models used some old components. Examples have been seen with hand or cocking levers, without strengthening fences or fillets. Also the calibre, No. 3, was not marked on these very early models as the difference in size of loading hole was so obvious compared with the .177 (No. 1) calibre size.

Quite a few of these large calibre rifles were made in Light Pattern length of 39″. This was due to certain export requirements. India, for example, would only allow the importation of air rifles if they could be classed as toys. The British Board of Trade through the India Office, managed to classify as Toys and, therefore, free of import restrictions, the "Britannia, Light and Heavy Gem, the Millita and the BSA Air Rifle in Ladies Pattern" as they incorrectly described it. Any orders received, therefore, from India had to be supplied in Light pattern regardless of calibre. This rather restrictive ruling was later to be amended to include all patterns and lengths of BSA rifles.

The light pattern 39″ models must have been very poor performers due to their short stroke pistons. The velocities must have been very low and the efficiency on live targets poor.

Even the standard length .250″ calibre rifles measuring 43¼″ in length were really not up to standard even when fitted with springs of round section, more powerful wire. So high was the trajectory of these weapons with the heavy .250″ pellet that an extra high rearsight leaf or bar was fitted to these rifles to enable them to be used at normal sporting ranges of up to 50 yards as advertised.

A single shot bolt action .22 long rifle sporting rifle was introduced by BSA in mid.

1908. This rifle was fitted with a very sturdy rearsight, having a large diameter central spring loaded elevation screw. As the sight was higher than the Improved Model D rearsight, it was ideal for the long pattern .250″ calibre BSA Air Rifle and the later rifles of this No. 3 bore were fitted with this new BSA sight. The same design of sight, with minor variations, was later fitted to all post Great War BSA air rifles.

By serial number 21150, BSA had lengthened the cylinder on some .250″ rifles to accommodate a longer, more powerful mainspring of 33 coils of .136 diameter size wire. The total length was now 45½″ and the figure 3 denoting the calibre was stamped on the breech. This extra power made the big rifles very effective indeed but still sales were not as great as anticipated, especially overseas where with the early short rifles the performance was so disappointing. One other factor which seriously affected sales was the limited availability of pellets of the larger calibre, particularly overseas where the cost of importing these pellets made them almost as dear as .22 rimfire or Morris Tube ammunition.

All of the .250″ calibre rifles had breech plug retaining plates, still with the large diameter peg and compensating spring but now marked P. Pat. with the Patent Number 8246/06 imprinted underneath in a straight line (see Plate 22).

According to known examples of these No. 3 bore rifles, the highest known serial number is 28013 which left the BSA factory in October, 1909. Only about 2,000 rifles were made and they were very slow indeed selling; most were despatched in late 1909 up to Autumn 1910. Some even left the factory in late 1914, having been in stock for 6½ years. Hardly the sales record of a market leader!!

As well as the reasons detailed to explain the poor selling rate of the .250″ model, there was another factor, created deliberately by BSA themselves. Before introducing the .250″ calibre rifle, they had already marketed a Standard pattern rifle in .22 calibre which proved to perform far better in the field than the .250″ model.

It should be noted that .250″, .22, .177, Standard and Light Pattern were all being assembled at the same period by BSA. There were only very short production runs of any one calibre or type. Records confirm that most .250″ calibre rifles were assembled to order. The 39″ models were made in very small quantity, the majority of .250″ models being evenly divided between 43½″ and 45½″ models. Both straight and Pistol hand stocks were supplied. A large number of No. 3 rifles were supplied with the BSA No. 12 aperture rearsight fitted to the trigger block. Over two thirds of these big calibre air rifles were exported.

With the regard to the accurate identification of models it has been found that it is almost impossible to identify an exact date or serial number at which a model change occurred. Reference has already been made to the practice of utilising existing components alongside the introduction of improved or modified components. For example, rifles having all the improved model modifications may be found which are marked ''The BSA Air Rifle (Lincoln Jeffries Patent)''. Rifles having full improved Model 'B' characteristics will be found with air cylinders marked ''The BSA Air Rifle'' and likewise rifles with improved Model 'D' characteristics will be found impressed with the legend ''The BSA Air Rifle (Improved Model 'B')''.

PLATE 35 *(G. Kerry)*
Special Rearsight fitted to the Juvenile Pattern Air Rifle Improved Model 'D'.
Fixed Leaf is marked for ten yards and Folding Leaf is marked for twenty yards.

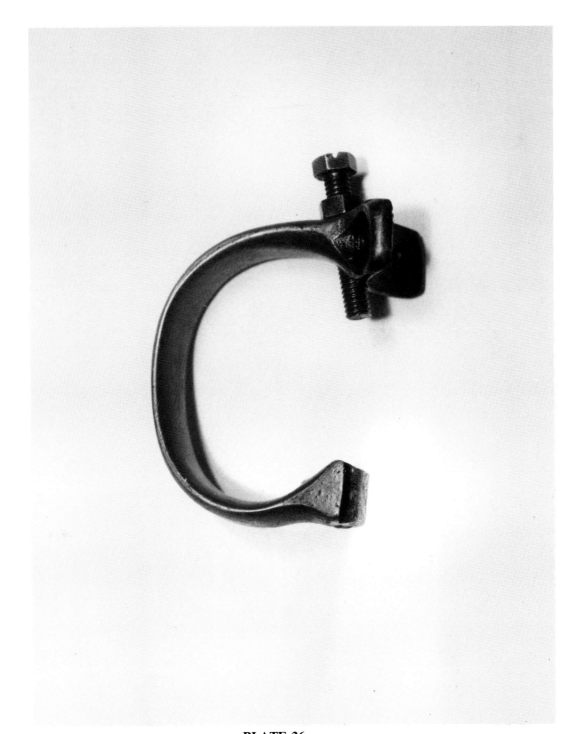

PLATE 36 *(G. Kerry)*
Improved Pattern Trigger Guard with Rear Dovetail Fitting. Mid 1913. Improved Model 'D'.

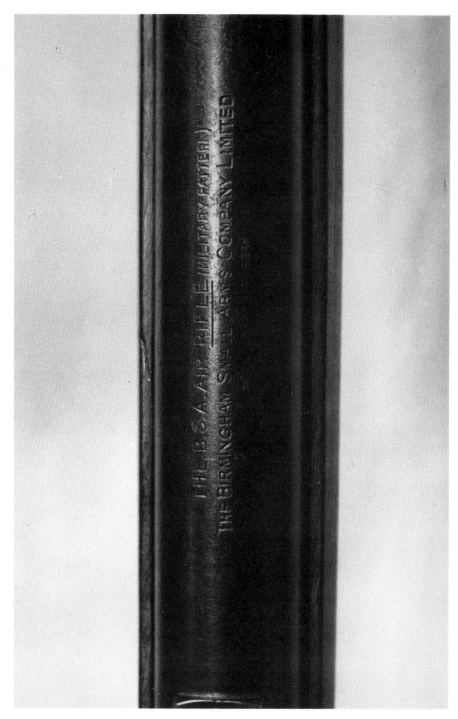

PLATE 37 *(G. Kerry)*
Cylinder markings of the BSA Military Pattern Air Rifle, First and Second Pattern.

Chapter 11

TOWARDS THE end of 1908, the final but one batch of Lincoln rifles was being assembled and these will be considered in due course. Meanwhile, the first prototype .22 air rifles were produced by BSA in mid 1908. First recorded number is 19025. These rifles were really a .22 version of the BSA Standard air rifle of 43¼" overall length. Only very few were made initially whilst the larger .250" Sporting Pattern was being developed.

In the Autumn of 1908, the BSA Company Ltd., was still fully engaged in arms production and in September, it was reported that the working week in the factory was being reduced from 53 to 48 hours a week, due to fall off in Government contracts. At that date, the BSA Company employed over 3,000 men at their Small Heath factory alone. The BSA Air Rifle (Improved Model D) was being produced as stated in .177" Standard and Light Pattern, .22" and .250" up to early December, 1908.

In August of that year, BSA started production of the penultimate batch of 'H The Lincoln' Patent 1904/5 air rifles for which they had been holding specialist components such as cylinders and trigger blocks for some considerable time. Lincoln Jeffries had already been allocated the serial numbers for this batch which ran from No. 22530 up to 23529, a total of 1,000 rifles. Although most of these rifles were finished before the end of 1908 (see Plate 51), it was several years before all of this batch left the BSA factory. Delivery was in fact spread over five years, the last models being despatched in November 1913. Eight rifles from this batch were in fact finished as BSA Improved Model D rifles between 1910 and 1913 and sold by BSA themselves.

From examples of this particular batch which have survived, there is a large number of very unorthodox models which appear to be made up from any spare parts that were handy at the time.

Most of the usual 'H The Lincoln Air Rifle' models are fairly orthodox but the cylinder inscription is amended to read 'H The Lincoln Air Rifle Patent 8761-04', they nearly all have a large letter 'L' impressed beneath the serial number. All bore the, by then, standard breech plug fastening system of the knurled nut and compensating spring. Most have BSA type Improved Model D trigger guards with the large diameter rear peg. They also have the Improved Model D type of hand or cocking lever with the strengthening fillets but several models have been noticed with the top of the cylinder drilled with a small hole almost ½" from the edge of the trigger block. This corresponds with a threaded hole in the threaded portion of the trigger block itself. Improved Model D rifles of BSA manufacture have also been seen with this peculiarity which purpose was to accept an extra lock screw between the trigger block and cylinder to enable the new BSA Model 12, Aperture rearsight to be fitted (see Plate 23).

PLATE 38 *(G. Kerry)*
Two Pre Great War Training Rifles.
Left—A Long Lee-Enfield Territorial Pattern Service Rifle showing the Morris Tube Adaptor
removed.
Right—A Long Lee-Enfield Carbine converted to .22 Long Rifle Calibre.

PLATE 39 *(G. Kerry)*
Pre Great War Ammunition used for training purposes.
Left to right—Full sized .303 Service Cartridge; Morris Tube .297/.230 Cartridge;
Rim Fire .220″ Long Rifle Cartridge; Adder .177″ Air Rifle Pellet.

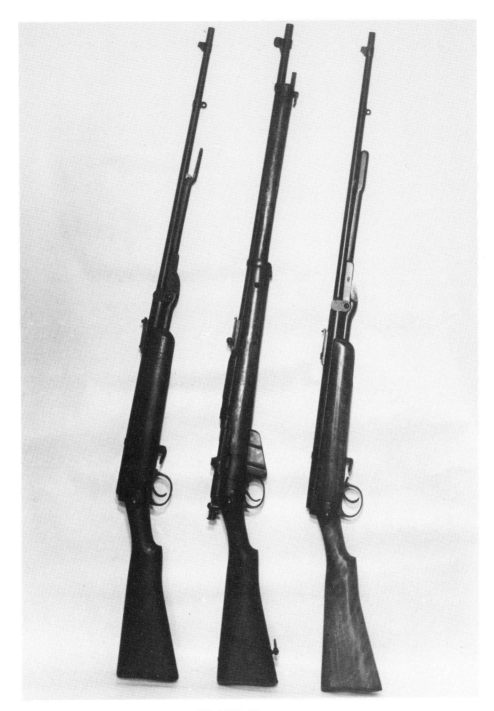

PLATE 40 *(G. Kerry)*
Left to Right—First Pattern BSA Military Pattern Air Rifle; Long Lee-Enfield Territorial Pattern
Service Rifle in .303 Calibre; Third Pattern BSA Military Pattern Air Rifle.

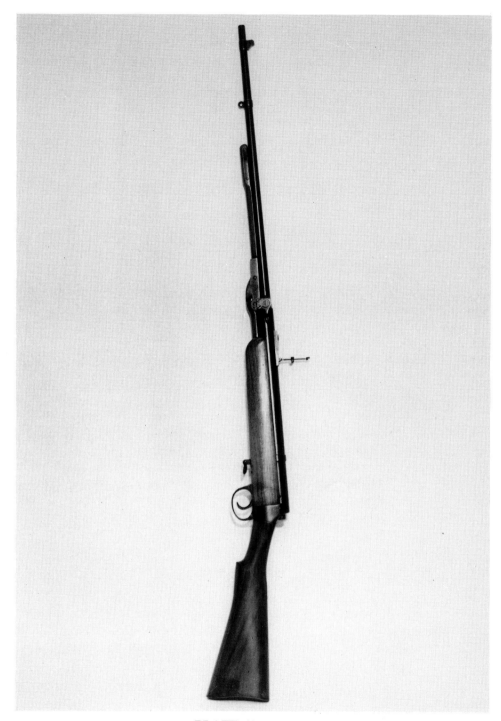

PLATE 41 *(G. Kerry)*
Military Pattern Air Rifle Third Batch showing Rearsight in elevated position.

Chapter 12

ONE PROBLEM of the screw-in trigger block system was a tendency for the front trigger guard fixing screws to become loose, allowing play between the trigger block and cylinder. This was of no consequence in a rifle with normal open sights fitted on the barrel but when an aperture sight was fitted to the trigger block, any movement between the trigger block and cylinder was detrimental to accuracy.

One BSA Air Rifle (Improved Model D) serial number 22075, which was fitted with a model 12 aperature sight, had a domed headed, countersunk screw, locking the trigger block to the cylinder at the position described. Two Lincoln rifles of the same period of manufacture, Nos. 23390 and 23490, also had the same locking screw fitted. A later rifle, however, No. 23474, did not have the cylinder drilled for the locking screw but the trigger block of this rifle was drilled and tapped to accommodate such a screw.

An even stranger rifle is No. 23628 (Improved Model D) which is fitted with a BSA (Improved Model 'B') type trigger guard with the small diameter rear fixing peg and a side button cocking lever catch not patented by Lincoln Jeffries until late 1910. The cocking lever could, of course, be a later replacement. The breech plug on this rifle was of the BSA type and is marked P. Pat. 8246/06 in a circular design, indicating that yet another improvement had taken place regarding the breech plug fastening plate (see Plate 52). To ensure more positive indexing of the breech plug in the open and closed positions, the projecting stud on the plate had been reduced in size and a spring loaded plunger fitted into the plug itself located into two indents on the plate. The large compensating spring became unnecessary as sufficient pressure could be applied to the plug by the plunger spring alone (see Plate 14).

As well as producing this penultimate batch of rifles for Lincoln Jeffries, BSA were promoting the new .22 calibre Sporting Air Rifle. Already pellets were being advertised under the brand name of Adder. These were made by Nobel Industries Ltd., at the old Adderley Park Rolling Mills in Birmingham. BSA were now distributing these pellets and were advertising them in all their current literature.

In August, 1909, a BSA advertisement appeared in *The Sporting Goods Review and the Gunmaker,* for the new powerful .22 bore BSA Air Rifle introduced for sporting purposes. The Adder Pellets in the same calibre were also promoted. The .22 Sporting Air Rifle was now in full production. To give increased performance and also to use up some of the long cylinders made specially for the later pattern .250″ rifles, the .22

version was now made longer than the previous few rifles which were just .22 calibre barrels on the Standard 43¼" ordinary pattern rifle. These new .22 rifles were 2" longer overall, being 45¼". The first of these long .22 air rifles was made by converting a rifle which was sent out as a 43¼" version at the end of June 1909, and was returned for credit for some reason, possibly because it did not develop the power advertised. It was converted by having a longer cylinder fitted together with a spring developing more power. It was found that the mainspring from the Military Pattern suited this rifle admirably.

It was reported in the trade journals that BSA were doing excellent business with its new No. 2 (.22) Air Rifle, particularly in Australia, America and South Africa. The rifle could be used for many other purposes besides target shooting practice. It was a resounding success as a sporting rifle as it had double the energy of the No. 1 (.177) rifle. The velocity of both rifles was the same whilst the No. 2 pellet is 15 grains compared with the No. 1 pellet at 8 grains. The big No. 2 (.22) Standard was advertised in Pistol Hand version only (see Plate 24), although some were fitted with straight hand stocks to special order (see Plate 59).

BSA announced a new aperture sight in January 1910. Called the No. 8 it was of folding construction with a large diameter eye piece. As an optional extra, the eye piece could be supplied with a six aperture revolving element to allow a choice of iris size. The sight was adjustable for elevation and windage and could be fitted on other BSA weapons as well as the air rifle range (see Plate 25, 60 and 61).

For the past six months, air rifle production had been running at a very high level but the air rifle business was still only a very small proportion of the Company's total business. Government work in early 1910 was not too plentiful and in a bid to increase air rifle sales even further, the BSA designers had been hard at work designing a rifle which would sell to, as yet, a new, untapped market. Young boys aged 10-15 years.

The new rifle was called the Junior Pattern of the BSA Improved Air Rifle. It turned out to be a diminutive version of the Light Pattern rifle. It was announced in January that the Junior would have a 11¼" stock and would be 5¼ lbs. in weight. That was all the information that the Trade was given. In the same editorial, a quite substantial price reduction was announced. The straight hand stock version of the standard and light pattern had been reduced from 45/- to 40/-. The pistol hand stock version of these rifles and including the big .22 calibre Standard, had been reduced in price from 50/- to 45/-. This price reduction had an immediate effect on sales which increased considerably, however, as often happens in such cases, in February BSA were awarded a very large contract to supply 60,000 .310 calibre Cadet Martini Action rifles for the Australian Government. These rifles were sold off to private purchasers between the wars and many of them are still used today for pest control work. Proof enough of the quality of BSA workmanship and materials. This Australian order was very welcome to BSA due to the very reduced Government contracts they were being awarded.

One interesting result of this quiet period in general production and active period in development, was the launching in April 1910 of a BSA Report Silencer at 17/- (85 pence). This was a very efficient sound moderator to be fitted to sporting and target rifles of .22 long rifle calibre. It was easily stripped for cleaning and had a lightweight aluminium body. Two versions were available, one had screw fitting to the barrel, the other had a screw operated pinch collar. No-one in 1910 had yet felt it necessary to fit a sound moderator to an air rifle! That sales gimmick was to come many years later.

The first Junior air rifles left the factory in early January 1910 and by April, orders were pouring into the works for this new weapon. Its immediate success can be attributed in no small measure by its attractive price of 40/- with a straighthand stock and 45/- with a pistol hand stock. Not surprisingly, most of the sales were for the straight hand stock version.

The small rifle did not turn out exactly as originally announced; it was ¼ lb. heavier. Made in .177 (No. 1) bore only the rifle was 2 lbs. lighter than the standard .22. Having an overall length of 34¼″, the barrel was only 14½″ long and the stock a tiny 11¼″ (see Plate 26).

The rifle was obviously made using as many standard parts as possible. The barrel, breech and cylinder of the Light Pattern was reduced by cutting 2″ from the muzzle end and recutting the foresight dovetail. The same cocking assembly, breech plug, piston, mainspring and trigger assembly as the Light Pattern was used. The only non-standard components were a smaller stock and smaller steel butt plate. In actual fact, the new Junior could be decribed as a Light Pattern cut off at either end (see Plate 27).

As with all BSA models the date of production have no relation whatsoever to the sequence of serial numbers. The lowest recorded number of a Junior is 28789, which was despatched on 11th July, 1910. However, one of the first batch of Junior rifles sent our from BSA was number 29593, despatched as part of a large order on 14th January, 1910.

PLATE 42 *(G. Kerry)*
Military Pattern Air Rifle Third Batch.

PLATE 43 *(G. Kerry)*
Cylinder and Trigger Block markings on the BSA Military Pattern Air Rifle Third Pattern.

PLATE 44 *(G. Kerry)*
Dummy Bolt on the BSA Military Pattern Air Rifle Third Pattern.

Chapter 13

IN AUGUST, 1911, BSA published a 63 page illustrated booklet entitled *"The Book of the BSA Air Rifle"*. This gave full details of the complete range of BSA Air Rifles and had sections on pellets, sights, targets, accessories etc., including instructions on building a range and starting an Air Rifle Club. As well as an advertising leaflet, it was also a complete and comprehensive guide to airgun shooting (see Plate 28).

During the whole of the year 1911, all models of the BSA Air Rifle were selling very well. Export business was also increasing, particularly for the large .22 calibre air rifle.

The same, however, could not be said for the sales of air rifles marketed by Mr. Lincoln Jeffries. From contemporary advertisements it would appear that the business of Lincoln Jeffries & Co. Ltd. was being operated from the same address as The Hercules Welding Company at 35 Whittall Street, Birmingham. The business of G. Lincoln Jeffries & Co. of 121 Steelhouse Lane, was still in being but the sale and servicing of the Lincoln Air Rifle were being carried out at the Whittall Street address. In January, 1911, *The Sporting Goods Review and The Gunmaker,* carried a quarter page advertisement for both Whittall Street businesses. The Hercules Welding Company specialised in welding broken cycle, motor and gun fittings. They were capable of repairing parts of cast iron, steel or aluminium. Their speciality was, however, the repair of gunparts.

The air rifle side of the business in the same advertisement was promoting "The Lincoln" patent air rifle stating that it "has no rival" also it is "also sold as BSA". Great emphasis is made of the fact of the origin of the rifle as the advertisement goes on to state "Inventor of the Lincoln Patent Air Rifle in three calibres, No. 1, 2 and 3 Price 45/- and 55/- each". These prices were published a year after BSA had reduced the price of their rifles to 45/- and 50/- respectively. This big difference in price would not have helped the Lincoln Jeffries sales drive, particularly as a Junior version of this design of rifle was now in the BSA range at only 40/- and 45/-.

The Lincoln Jeffries advertisement also confirms that a quantity of .22 calibre "Lincoln" air rifles were supplied in the batch made by BSA in 1908/9 and also that the 98 rifles finished by BSA in August and September, 1908 in the fifth batch of Lincoln rifles, serial numbers 10410 to 10507, were in the large .250″ No. 3 bore calibre.

A final, small quantity of rifles were assembled and despatched by BSA as Lincoln air rifles, starting in August, 1910 and finishing in November 1913. A total 260 rifles were involved, calibre unknown, the bulk of which was despatched in late 1911. Amongst this 260 rifles was an additional 21 rifles made and finished as BSA Air Rifles all in .177 calibre as Light patterns. Despatch of these was between April 1911 and August 1912. The serial numbers for this final batch of Lincoln air rifles ran from 35030-35311. All the serial numbers had the identification letter 'L' stamped beneath the number sequence.

Possibly due to the inability of Lincoln Jeffries to be able to take up his allocated quantity of Lincoln rifles, a quantity of 219 serial numbers was never issued as the numbers 35312 to 35529 were not completed in the registers.

The year of 1911 was a good production year for BSA as far as air rifle manufacture was concerned. All models were selling well and the sale of the new Junior model was so good that it warranted a comment in the Trade Press in July on how satisfactory sales for this new model were progressing.

Towards the end of the year, air rifle sales were so increased and Government contracts from our own and foreign countries were being granted to BSA that the work force was increased by almost one third to nearly 4,000. With this abundance of work, the inevitable happened and in late September, the whole work force came out on strike for a pay increase of 1/- (5 pence) per week. The strike was instigated by 500 union men walking out demanding the pay increase. They were followed by the rest of the work force, reportedly in sympathy, but more likely, because the 500 skilled union men brought production to a standstill. The BSA Company was reported to have agreed to the 1/- per week increase but in return, wanted the working week increased from 50 to 52 hours. The strike was settled satisfactorily in December of 1911. If the work force got the coveted 1/- a week, or if the Company got its extra two hours a week, is not recorded.

The various models of BSA Air Rifles were now finding a world wide market. In October, 1911, the range of rifles was awarded a Grand Prix at the Turin Sports Goods Exhibition. BSA were now finding that direct advertising was really showing results as regards sales. In addition to their publication *"The Book of the BSA Air Rifle"*, released in August, a few months previously the Company had printed a small brochure on their range of air rifles to be given away by distributors. This, too, was proving very popular and leading to many enquiries.

Mr. Lincoln Jeffries had for over a year been busy on improving his air rifle design, two major improvements which he developed were given patents in 1911, having been perfected during 1910.

Both these improvements were to be used commercially by BSA and also helped in a very minor way to alleviate some of the financial difficulties of Lincoln Jeffries & Co. Ltd. in the following year.

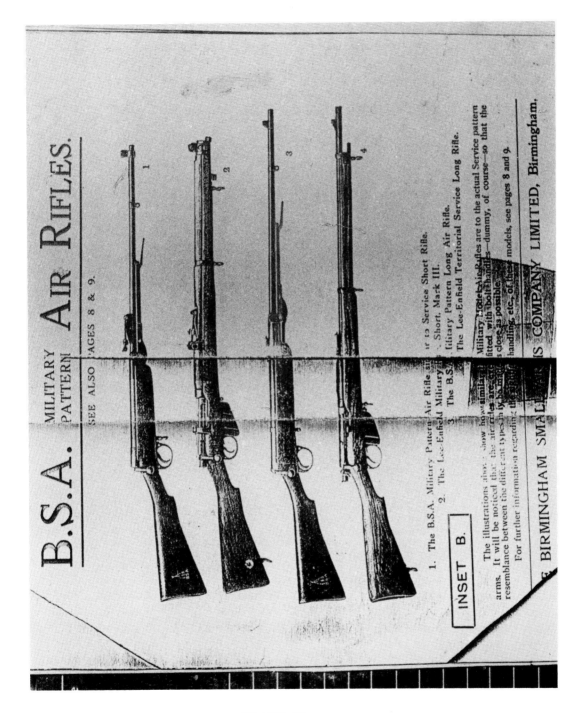

PLATE 45 *(G. Kerry)*
Details of the Long and Short Pattern Military Air Rifles advertised in the BSA Catalogue of 1911.
No example of the Short Pattern Rifle is known to exist.

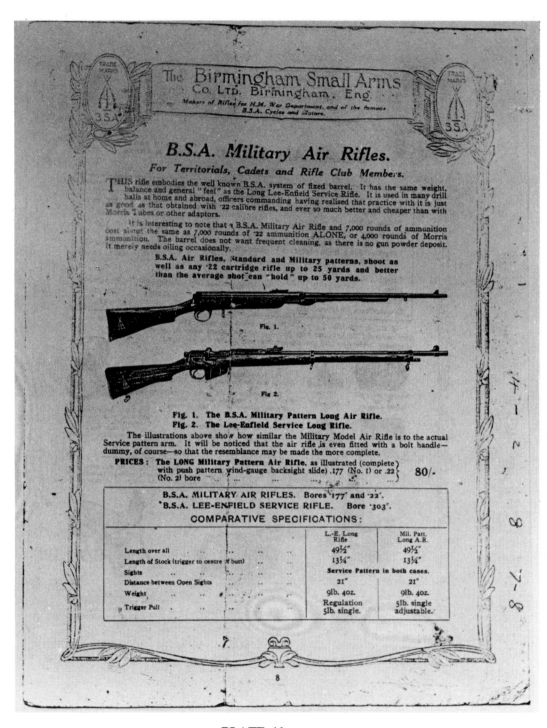

PLATE 46 *(G. Kerry)*
The Third Pattern BSA Military Air Rifle detailed in the 1913 BSA Catalogue.

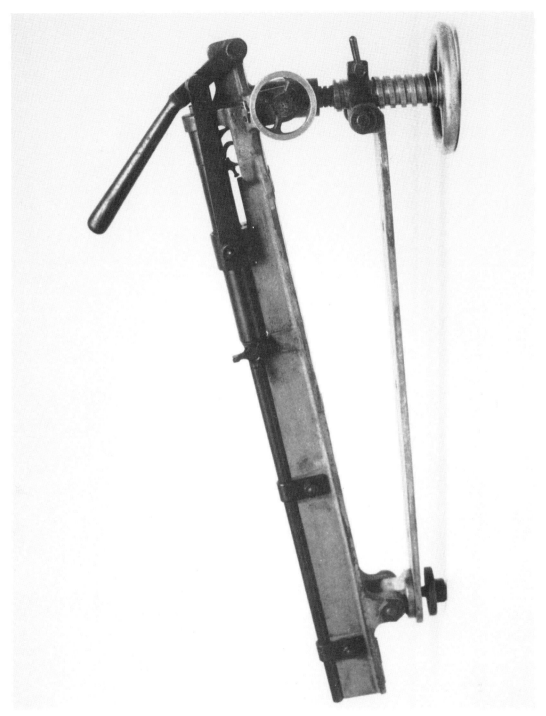

PLATE 47 *(Eddie Barber)*
The BSA Gun Laying Teacher, Land Pattern.

PLATE 48 *(Eddie Barber)*
The BSA Gun Laying Teacher, Land Pattern, details of Elevation and Windage Screws.

98

Chapter 14

THE FIRST successful Lincoln Jeffries invention was an improved catch to the cocking lever or hand lever of his air rifle design. Instead of relying on a simple spring loaded plunger to retain the hand lever, this new design incorporated a positive mechanical fixture in the form of a spring loaded, thumb operated catch positioned on the side of the hand lever, which engaged into a ring shaped catch block fitted into the usual dovetail milled in the underside of the barrel. This improvement was covered by Patent 25783/10, granted on 7th September, 1911. It was used on production rifles by BSA from that date, its first introduction being around serial number 45,000 (see Plate 29).

The second improvement concerned the trigger mechanism of the Lincoln design. Several years previously, Mr. Lincoln Jeffries had noticed an aspect of the underlever cocking system which had always caused concern regarding safety. If a shooter was foolish enough to pull the trigger before the hand lever was returned to its closed position, or if the sear or piston rod became worn, making engagement uncertain, then the hand lever could close violently as the piston came forward. If the shooter's hand was on the lever or barrel when this happened, quite serious injury could result. Both BSA and Lincoln Jeffries printed warnings of this peculiarity of the underlever system in their various brochures and leaflets; but still accidents occurred.

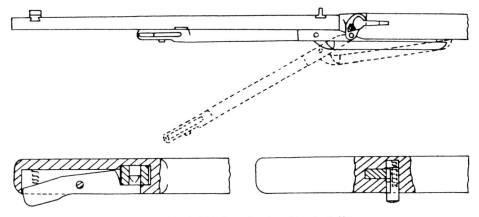

Patent 25783 of 1910. Part drawing. Lincoln Jeffries.

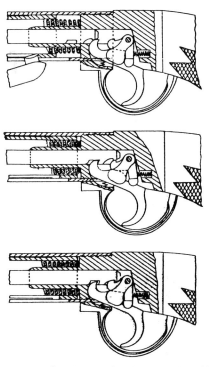

Patent 30338 of 1910. Part drawing. Lincoln Jeffries.

During 1910, Mr. Lincoln Jeffries had invented a trigger mechanism which obviated the accidental slippage of the sear/piston rod engagement. He produced a safety device in the form of a supplementary, or double sear, which engaged a second bent in the piston rod (see Plate 30). This double sear arrangement prevented any accidental discharging of the air rifle as the trigger was required to be positively pulled to release the piston. Allocated patent number 30338/10, the application was accepted in October 1911. It was used on production rifles by BSA from the spring of 1913 (see Plate 31). In practice this design proved to be a failure as far as the safety aspect was concerned. So as to use up the hundreds of parts made, the second sear was rivetted to the main sear assembly (see Plate 30).

In the Autumn of 1911, a new advertising campaign by BSA started in the Trade Press to encourage dealers to carry stocks of BSA rifles, Adder pellets and accessories in preparation for the Winter Air Rifle Shooting Season as the National Air Rifle Championships to be held at that time would be offering big money prizes and would encourage the formation of new clubs and attract new competitors to the sport.

In December 1911, BSA directed even greater advertising at the Trade. Dealers were encouraged to hold stocks for intended Christmas presents. The advertising was directed particularly at what BSA termed "The Apathetic Dealer" who only ordered when he received a firm inquiry and did not carry stocks of the full range of BSA air rifles.

At the close of 1911, sales were beginning to slow down and BSA were obviously concerned particularly as current military and Government contracts were almost completed with no repeat orders in the pipeline.

100

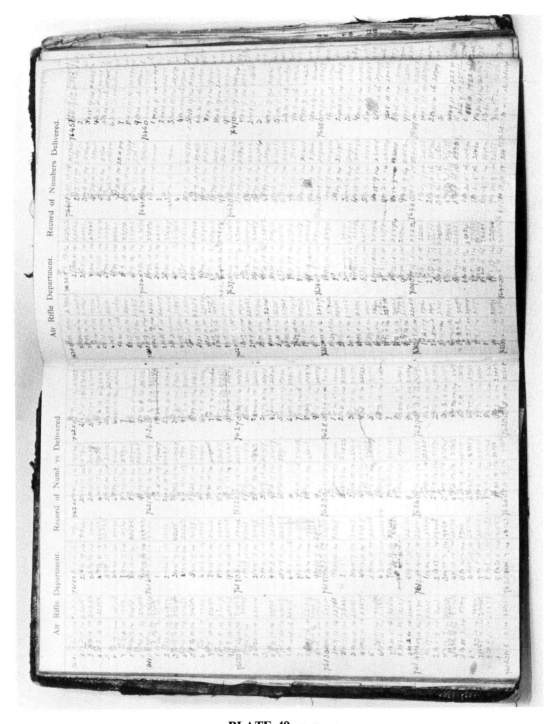

PLATE 49 *(G. Kerry)*
One of the Pre Great War handwritten ledgers from the Air Rifle Warehouse of BSA Guns Ltd.

PLATE 50 *(G. Kerry)*
Six sizes of BSA Air Rifles: Left to Right—Military Pattern, Sporting Pattern .22,
Standard Pattern .177, Light Pattern .177, Juvenile Pattern .177, Junior Pattern .177.

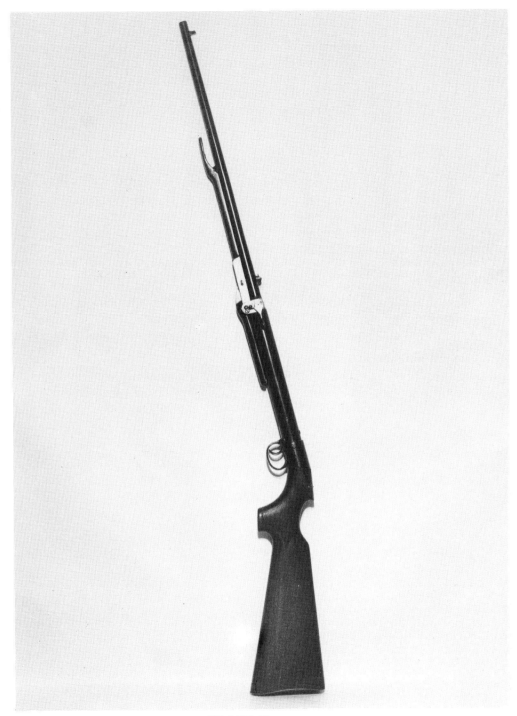

PLATE 51 *(G. Kerry)*
'H The Lincoln Air Rifle' from Seventh Batch, approx. 1908.

PLATE 52 *(G. Kerry)*
Improved Breech Plug and Retaining Plate with Indexing Plunger & Spring. Late Pattern.

Chapter 15

ONE OF THE first announcements in the Trade Press at the start of 1912, was the sad statement that the business of Lincoln Jeffries & Co. Ltd. was to be sold. The business, stock and plant were offered for sale but the goodwill had at the time of the advertisement already been purchased by a firm who preferred to remain anonymous. The reason for the sale was given as the wish of Mr. Lincoln Jeffries to retire. He was, at that time, 65 years old and the announcement stated that he intended to spend his final years in New Zealand, which country he had chosen because of its agreeable climate.

On February 28th, an extraordinary general meeting of shareholders of Lincoln Jeffries & Co. Ltd. confirmed a resolution adopted on 12th February, that the company should be put into voluntary liquidation. Mr. George Lincoln Jeffries was appointed his own liquidator. A creditor's meeting was arranged for March 14th. The Birmingham Small Arms Co. Ltd. were the largest creditor at that time. The previously mentioned mysterious purchaser of the Company's goodwill was Mr. George Lincoln Jeffries. This goodwill was afterwards transferred to his wife and three sons. It is very possible, but not yet confirmed, that part of the settlement concerning the large debt to BSA was the transfer of all of the Lincoln Jeffries patents to the Company. Up until mid 1912, the hand or cocking levers with side button catches all carried on their underside the inscription "Lincoln Jeffries Patents 8761-04 25783-10 R^d 479972''. After this period towards the end of 1912, production rifles were fitted with hand levers bearing the inscription "BSA Patents 8761-04 25783-10 R^d 479972'' (see Plate 32). Unfortunately, no records of this period from either company survive so how the patents were acquired by BSA is purely a matter of conjecture. It is, however, a fact that not only the two aforementioned patents, but also No. 30338-10 covering the double safety sear granted to Lincoln Jeffries, was actually put into production in early 1913 as a BSA patent.

The new, more positive, side button hand lever catch covered by Lincoln Jeffries Patent 25783/10 had been introduced into BSA air rifle production by October 1911 and by early 1912 stocks of snap fastening bayonet style hand levers were all used up. After this period, any old model rifles accepted for repair were fitted with the new type hand lever and ring catch block. These replacements account for some very early rifles of both BSA and Lincoln Jeffries models with this later hand lever assembly. A quantity of early pattern hand levers were retained to complete assembly of 'H The Lincoln' Air Rifles still not supplied against the original Lincoln Jeffries contract.

Towards the end of 1911, production of the Junior Rifle ceased as sufficient had been made to satisfy the anticipated Christmas trade of that year. Production restarted in March 1912 and generally assembly during that year was steady but not great. All patterns and calibres were being assembled at the same time. Sufficient components were made for Junior rifles during this year that they were still being despatched at the end of 1914, one year after a completely new lighter weight model Junior or Juvenile pattern model had been perfected.

In November 1912, BSA mounted its biggest advertising campaign ever by taking full page advertisements in both Trade Journals. Not only were air rifles promoted but also .22 cartridge Sporting rifles, both standard and a special folding pocket model; .410 Shotguns which were built on modified long Lee Enfield actions and barrels but also the now very comprehensive range of sights was mentioned, together with rifles and guns made to special order. To give more encouragement to dealers to stock up for the Christmas trade, BSA produced special "Christmas Present" illustrated booklets and promotional Christmas Window Show cards to be used by retailers to attract additional Christmas business.

This special sales effort was necesssary not only to encourage the sale of sporting weapons of all types but to find sufficient orders to keep the work force, which was already by November 1912, on short time. As is always the case with any privately owned arms or ammunition plant relying heavily on Government contracts; in times of emergency their skills are at a premium but as was the case in 1912, the whole Empire was at peace and to survive the factories had to make a variety of products to keep the work force together.

In the history of BSA, the factory have made bicycles, shoetrees, cigarette cases, horse shoes, roller skates, motorcycles, cars and even radio sets in order to provide employment in lean peace time periods. Kynochs, the Birmingham Munitions Company of similar age to BSA, have been forced to make even more bizarre products, such as soap, candles, machine bearings, air rifles, bicycles, fountain pens and even lipstick cases and toy cartridges for children's guns during similar slack periods. The W. W. Greener Company's peacetime diversifications were even stranger; included amongst which were cream making machines, grapefruit knives, fishermen's pen knives, military swords, air rifles, bicycles and motorcycles, pistol bayonets and violin bow resin to name but a few.

During 1912, the designs of all of the air rifles in production were standardized and the large .22 calibre model was named (for production purposes) the BSA Air Rifle No. 2 Mk. II. The cylinder length was specified as 10⅜″ and the mainspring was changed from one piece to a pair of opposingly coiled round section wire springs of 17 coils each. These springs were not only easier and cheaper to produce but certainly produced more power in the large sporting air rifle.

The .177 Standard rifle was renamed "The BSA Air Rifle Ordinary Pattern Mk. II No. 1 Bore". Cylinder length was 8½″ and the pair of oval wire mainsprings left and right hand coiled each of 21 coils, were specified. This is the original mainspring combination as developed back in 1907. The "Mk. II" part of the new description referred to the side button catch type hand lever.

The BSA Air Rifle in all its forms had become accepted world wide. In America, the air rifle was being recognised as a serious weapon, even by gun happy pioneer spirited Americans. A Mr. E. C. Crossman, a writer for an American Sporting magazine, was sent a BSA Air Rifle to test and he declared it "... the dangdest looking Figi war-club that ever got into a catalogue". He reported that he used the air rifle to shoot at a trespassing chicken in his garden. He killed it and put its death down to sunstroke! Mr. Crossman's chicken slaughtering article certainly launched the air rifle in America. Following its publication, demand for all types of the BSA Air Rifle increased. In September 1912, at the Company's A.G.M. the steady growth of sales for the BSA Air Rifle was mentioned, particularly its growing popularity in America.

Towards the end of the year, it was reported that sales of BSA rifles of all types had been exceptional for the Christmas Trade, both home and overseas. In Australia and New Zealand all models were selling well. The money invested by BSA in their new advertising campaigns was now beginning to pay off.

The BSA Air Rifle was attracting attention in more exclusive circles; published in *"Arms and Explosives"* magazine, under the monthly section "Lectures to Young Gunmakers", the trigger mechanism of the BSA Air Rifle was discussed in detail. Acknowledged as a development of Mr. Lincoln Jeffries, it was reported that 50,000 air rifles with the standard trigger mechanism had been produced up to April 1912. The article praised the workmanship and materials used in BSA air rifle production pointing out that in the Standard Pattern model, the springs exerted a force of 140-150 lbs. pressure on the trigger when the rifle was cocked, yet it required only 5 lbs. to let if off. Under the same method of measurement, a sporting shotgun has about 12 lbs. pressure on the sear.

In November 1912, BSA issued a new leaflet giving instructions on the use of the new side button catch hand lever. This was supplied to retailers to give away with any of the new model air rifles sold.

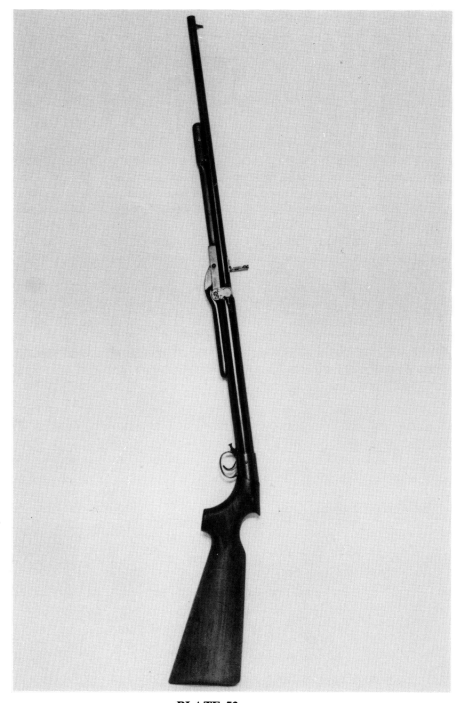

PLATE 53 *(G. Kerry)*
.22″ Improved Model 'D' with Double Safety Sear and No. 21 Rearsight fitted into
Barrel Dovetail.

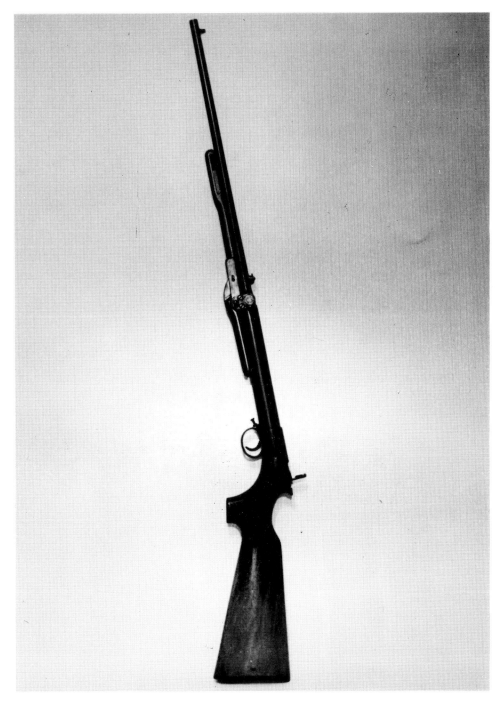

PLATE 54 *(G. Kerry)*
Light Pattern Improved Model 'D' with Double Safety Sear, Mark II Cocking Lever Catch and
No. 21b Aperture Sight fitted to stock.

PLATE 55 *(G. Kerry)*
The Last Pattern Improved Model 'D'.
Top—Standard or Ordinary Pattern; Bottom—Light Pattern.

Chapter 16

THE BEGINNING of 1913 saw sales of air rifles still at a satisfactory level maintained by the massive advertising campaign launched just before Christmas 1912. In January, the Company were fortunate to obtain an order for 45,000 military rifles, which guaranteed enough work for at least six months for the main work force.

During March, the patent double safety sear/trigger mechanism was introduced to air rifle production. It was first fitted to .22 calibre Mk. II rifles which were despatched during April against a large order for New Zealand. The prefix letter 'S' was added to the serial numbers of most rifles of whatever pattern fitted with this improved trigger mechanism. The patent number 30338-10 was also impressed on the left hand side of the trigger block above the serial number (see Plate 31). Not all rifles now in production were fitted with the new trigger modification. There was no definable period when all production was given 'S' prefix serial numbers and some rifles were produced fitted with the new safety sear mechanism but without the 'S' prefix to the serial number and the omission of the patent details from the trigger block. The first recorded fitting was to rifle number S 51985, which left BSA on the 25th April, 1913. The issue of serial numbers at this time was very erratic and the bulk of 1913 despatches did not, however, start until serial number 62000 and even after this, sales diminished considerably during the second half of the year. It is interesting to see from the despatch records that rifles of all patterns in the 62,000-63,000 series were despatched in 1912, 13, 14 and even 1915.

In March of 1913, assembly of Junior pattern rifles recommenced. Some of these were supplied with the new improved trigger system but the bulk were assembled with standard triggers. A few Junior rifles were fitted with the new side button cocking lever catches (see Plate 33). The majority of Junior production at this time was for stock in order to clear all components for this model from the stores to enable a new improved Junior or Juvenile rifle to be introduced as soon as possible, hopefully to improve air rifle sales generally.

This new rifle which was also marketed as a Junior Pattern was a completely new concept as far as BSA was concerned. Originally, this model was called the Juvenile Pattern but the title of Junior was now well established and associated with the small rifle already on the market; so the title "Junior" was retained for this new model also.

Another reason for the retention of the model name was due to the fact that at the time of intended introduction of the Juvenile model, there were still very considerable stocks of Junior models unsold in retail shops and in stock at the factory. To have promoted a new similar model type with a different name would have meant that the unsold stock of Junior rifles would have remained unsold. It was the great concern for the unsold stock of Junior rifles which decided the price reduction in August, ostensibly to boost the Christmas demand but to actually clear old stocks of Junior rifles. For identification purposes in this book, the second pattern Junior rifle will be referred to by the correct nomenclature of the "Juvenile Pattern".

The Juvenile was a daintier, more elegant rifle than the Junior (see Plate 34). Made in .177 calibre only, it had the improved side button catch lever and all models examined have been found to be fitted with the double safety sear/trigger assembly; although the records suggest that a quantity of rifles was made with standard pattern triggers. The cylinder was a standard length for the light pattern at $7\frac{1}{8}''$ long and was of much slimmer section that that of the Junior. It had an external bore of $1\frac{1}{8}''$ as opposed to the usual BSA air rifle external cylinder bore size of $1\frac{1}{4}''$. Consequently, the piston was much lighter. The piston washer was fitted with a single nut in early production models but normal piston washer standard screw fitting was also used and examples have been seen with the piston washer rivetted on to the piston by expanding the protruding end of the piston rod to secure the washer assembly. This last mentioned fitting could, however, be the work of some bungling amateur "gunsmith".

To enable the rifle to be cocked more easily by small children, the mainspring was reduced in power. The wire used was only .100″ diameter and the external diameter of the spring was reduced to .720″ with only 29 coils. Due to its reduced power, a special rearsight was fitted to the Juvenile model. The sight had a dovetailed base of $\frac{3}{4}''$ and had one fixed leaf marked 10 yards and a folding leaf for shooting at 20 yards (see Plate 35). The advertised effective range of the Junior rifle was the same as the light pattern—30 yards. It is, however, interesting to note that the effective range of the Light pattern quoted in the first BSA catalogue of 1907 was 50 yards! An instance perhaps of unintentional, exaggerated, poetic licence! Another exaggeration, or mistake this time, in the 1911 catalogue, gave the barrel length of the Junior rifle as $15\frac{1}{4}''$, whereas the actual length was $14\frac{1}{4}''$. The Juvenile Pattern was made with the same advertised length barrel as the Junior, $15\frac{1}{4}''$ and was described correctly this time in the descriptive leaflet featuring the new Juvenile Pattern published by BSA in August 1913. This leaflet quoted a price of 35/- for the Juvenile Pattern with straight hand stock and 40/- for the pistol hand version. The former was the cheapest rifle ever produced by BSA.

An interesting major component change in the Juvenile model was the rear fitting of the trigger guard. This was altered from a protruding, circular stud or peg, to a dovetail block; possibly for ease in machining. This modified form of trigger guard was used in all models at the same time as existing stocks were being used up, from mid 1913 onwards. Larger diameter, broader headed fixing screws were used in conjunction with this modified trigger guard (see Plate 36).

In September, a full advertising campaign was launched for the new Juvenile rifle advising the trade to stock up for the Christmas trade. It should be remembered that there were still quite substantial stocks of Junior rifles in the BSA stores at this time. No doubt many were sent out against orders for the newly advertised Juvenile Pattern. The lowest number Juvenile Pattern to be produced was No. 65442, despatched mid December 1912. The records suggest that the Company had intended to market the Junior and Juvenile as two separate models but confusion amongst the Trade and the Public resulted in general misunderstanding regarding exactly what model was required. Sales generally during the whole of 1913 were very disappointing. Had demand continued at the same level as during the previous year, 1912, than all the Junior models would have been sold before the intended introduction of the Juvenile model in late 1912, early 1913. But this perfect market state was not to be and the unexpectedly slow sales resulted in the sorry state of both small models being in stock at the same time.

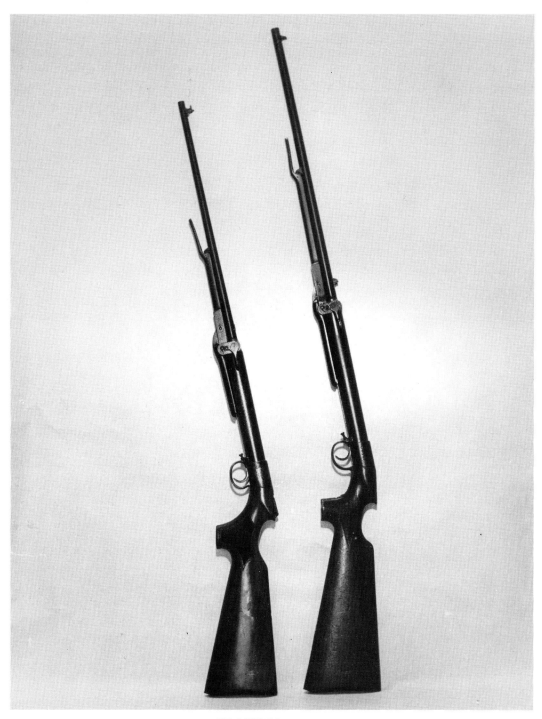

PLATE 56 *(G. Kerry)*
The Lincoln Air Rifle Standard Pattern, Right. Ladies Pattern, Left.

The Birmingham Small Arms
Co. Ltd. Birmingham. Eng
*Makers of Rifles for H.M. War Departments, and of the famous
B.S.A. Cycles and Motors.*

B.S.A. Air Rifles.

Patents No. 8761-1904, 8246-1906.   Rd. No. 479972.   Awarded Gold Medal, Christchurch.

Standard or Heavy Weight Pattern.
Pistol-hand stock, each 50/-   Straight-hand stock, each 45/-
'177 (No. 1) and '22 (No. 2) bores.

Light or Medium Weight Pattern.
Pistol-hand stock, each 45/-   Straight-hand stock, each 40/-
(.177 bore only).

Junior or Boy's Pattern.
Pistol-hand stock, each 40/- Straight-hand stock, each 35/-
(.177 bore only).

Illustration of Standard Pattern fitted with
Straight Hand Stock.

THE METHOD OF COCKING the
B.S.A. Air Rifle is here illustrated.
The patent form of lever mechanism
is used instead of the barrel as in other systems.

If fitted with **SLING SWIVEL ATTACHMENTS**   2 6 (per set of 2) each extra.
SLINGS—for '177 bore   -   -   2/6   '22 bore   -   -   2/6 each extra.
PISTON SPRINGS—'177 and '22 bore   1 6 each.   **SIGHT PROTECTORS**   1/- each.

The Pellet Chamber or Breech Plug.
Is operated by means of the lever shown.
After cocking the rifle it is turned into the
position shown in Fig 1. The Pellet is dropped,
round nose downwards, into the hole so exposed
and the lever is then turned back as in Fig 2.

Fig. 1.   Fig. 2.

6

PLATE 57 *(G. Kerry)*
The range of model sizes and styles detailed in the 1913 BSA Catalogue.

PLATE 58 *(G. Kerry)*
'L The Lincoln Air Rifle' with No 21a Aperture Sight and Target Foresight No. 20a.

Chapter 17

THE TWO Junior Pattern rifles were amongst the shortest lived models ever produced by BSA, only 1097 Juveniles were made, the last one being despatched from the factory in October 1914. This was the same month that the last Junior Pattern was despatched also. A total of just over 1,000 Junior rifles were produced by BSA but as so many were sent to overseas markets, they are discovered less often by British collectors than the later Juvenile pattern. In spite of very extensive research there is still considerable confusion regarding the actual intentions of BSA with regard to the intended characteristics of the Junior and Juvenile Pattern rifles.

A full size technical drawing exists of a small pattern air rifle designated "The BSA Air Rifle (Juvenile Patt.)" dated October 1911. Dimensionally, this is the same as the Junior rifle produced in that year but the drawing shows the side button type (Mark II) hand lever catch which, according to existing examples, was rarely fitted to the Junior rifle. An improved pillar type of rearsight is also specified, the same sight in fact developed for the .22 bolt action rifle of 1908 which was fitted to late production models of the No. 3 (.250") Improved Model D rifles. The drawing also specified a reduced length mainspring of 21¼" coils and keeper screws for the hand lever axis pin and the cocking link axis pin of the same size. In all aspects the rifle specified was as the light model except that the stock length was shorter.

The drawing was obviously for an intended improvement on the Junior Pattern model and indicated the recognised modifications which had been become evident from consumer reaction to the original Junior model, namely the improved cocking mechanism, modified rearsight and reduced mainspring strength all of which were catered for in the later Juvenile Pattern model.

In November 1913, BSA secured an order from the War Office to produce 30,000 Short Magazine Lee Enfield Service rifles Mk. III Pattern conversions for the British Army. This was followed in December by the commencement under licence of air and water cooled Lewis machine guns. This was the result of a previous contract to make barrels only for this machine gun in late 1912. The experimental department of BSA made a quantity of complete guns as a feasibility project and a BSA made Lewis Gun was demonstrated at Bisley in the summer of 1913. Samples of the new gun were taken to show overseas Governments and interest was shown and orders received from America, Sweden and Russia. As part of the sales team, the Barrel Mill Manager, Mr. Wykes, travelled by the famous 'Orient Express' train to Russia to demonstrate the new Lewis Gun to the Tzarist Imperial Army.

The Military side of BSA business was very healthy by the end of 1913, but in the following year air rifle production was to take a back seat when all energy was spent on preparation for the most unnecesssary slaughter in history, the Great War of 1914-18.

With the author having worked for many years in the Gun Trade, with part of the time being spent at the massive BSA Guns Ltd. plant at Shirley, it is easy to see how the barrel length of the Juvenile rifles differed in length from the first Junior, but was the same as the incorrectly advertised barrel length. When the Juvenile model was being conceived and the drawing for this model was being prepared, instead of actually measuring the barrel length of the current Junior model, it is possible that a brochure or catalogue was referred to by a busy draughstman and the printing mistake of 1911 resulted in the increased barrel length of the new model in 1913.

Generally, air rifle sales continued very slowly in early and mid 1914, but during this quiet period, development work was going ahead at the BSA factory. Plans were in hand to replace the well established Improved Model 'D' pattern with a new design of rifle to be called the BSA Air Rifle Standard Pattern. The most important modification was to fit an end push button catch to the cocking lever; the design of this was based on the BSA patent of 1906, Number 25830, accepted in August 1907, covering a hand disengaged spring loaded bolt or button on the end of the cocking lever which affected a solid and positive fastening to the underside of barrel so that sling swivels could be fitted to the lever itself.

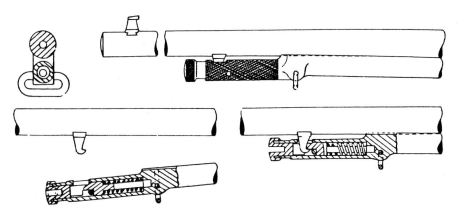

Patent 25830 of 1906. BSA.

Experiments were also undertaken in photo-etching model details on to the cylinder instead of the laborious and not very efficient method of rolling the model identification into the steel of the cylinder. Photo-etching would also facilitate individual model identification as details could be applied to the finished rifle after blacking, whereas previously, the model identification was impressed into the cylinder whilst the component was in the "white", unfinished state.

Photo-etching was used successsfully from mid 1914 onwards where rifle air cylinders which had not yet been mechanically impressed or engraved were used to build rifles for specific orders.

It will be seen from the serial number and data analysis at the end of this book, that it is not possible to identify an exact point in the serial number sequence at which photo-etching was introduced. Many air cylinders were impressed with the legend ''The BSA Air Rifle (Improved Model D)'' and were in store awaiting assembly until well after the end of the Great War. Early Standard Pattern Models in both .177 and .22 calibre are known as having cylinders impressed in this fashion but which were not assembled until late 1919 or even early 1920. Many low serial number Light Pattern Standard rifles carrying the familiar 'L' serial number prefix carry this pre war cylinder impression of (Improved Model D).

From mid 1914, air cylinders in the unimpressed state were assembled into rifles and then photo-etched, many with the generally accepted post Great War legend ''The BSA Air Rifle Standard Pattern No. 1 (.177) (or No. 2) (.22), Bore''.

The outbreak of the Great War saw a temporary cessation of air rifle production in October of 1914 and over 1,000 serial numbers were never issued between 78217 and 79529 although in September of that year assembly started again using those components which were already in stock and rifles were assembled and despatched through the duration of the war until nearly all the stock of components had been used up. This limited air rifle production during a war time period of great activity can be attributed to the opinion at the time that air rifle shooting helped to make future soldiers.

The rifles assembled in this manner during the Great War were mostly exact models in Light, Ordinary, Juvenile or Junior pattern but inevitably, many hybrid versions were produced which have caused much interest, confusion and argument amongst BSA enthusiasts and collectors for the last sixty years and which will no doubt continue to do so for many years to come.

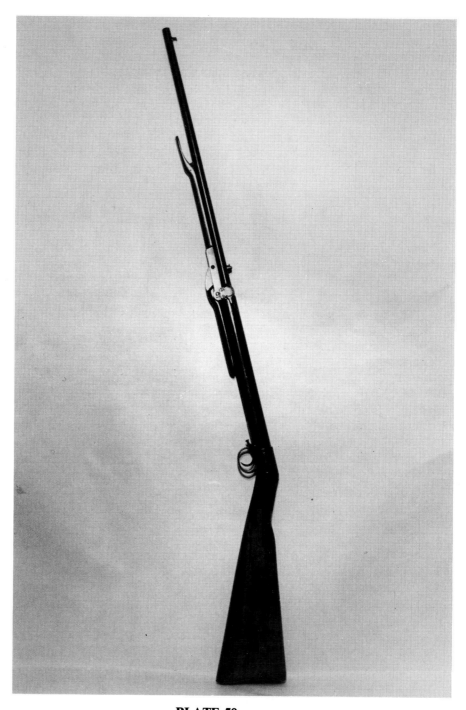

PLATE 59 *(G. Kerry)*
.22″ Improved Model 'D' 45½″ Long with Straight Hand Stock and Second Pattern Cocking Lever 1909.

PLATE 60 *(G. Kerry)*
Details of the BSA Aperture Rearsight No. 8a with 6 Hole Iris. Note the cutaway portion of the
Comb of the Stock, to accommodate the sight when folded.

PLATE 61 *(G. Kerry)*
An Improved Model 'D' .22 Calibre Sporting Air Rifle in its original fitted wooden box.
Note box of contemporary BSA No. 2 Air Rifle Pellets.

THE BSA MILITARY PATTERN RIFLES

Chapter 18

BRIEF REFERENCE has already been made to the introduction of a large military style of target rifle by BSA in the summer of 1907 at the Bisley Meeting. Referred to as "The BSA MILITARY PATTERN AIR RIFLE", this model was the forerunner of a quite amazingly complex range of models produced between 1907 and 1914, which until now have been classified under one heading as the "The BSA Military Pattern Air Rifle".

During the many years that this reference book has been researched, the most difficult and unrewarding part has been connected with this most fascinating development of the BSA Air Rifle. Very few production records have been discovered, only very minimal

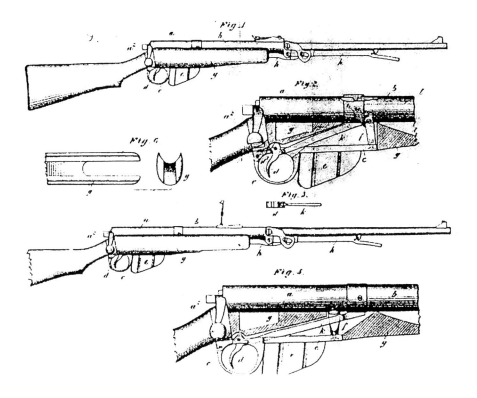

manufacturing details exist and few records of quantities or calibres manufactured, have survived. Only by studying registered patents, references in Trade Journals and other publications and examination and reference to existing examples of the many varieties of this most interesting of all the BSA Air Rifle modifications can some detailed history of the evolution of this model be compiled.

Early in 1906, Mr. Leslie Bown Taylor, Managing Director of Westley Richards in Birmingham in conjunction with Mr. C. Gardner, had modified the BSA air rifle cocking lever and breech plug system in such a way that the breech plug was automatically opened by the cocking stroke of the cocking or hand lever. This was achieved by a specially shaped link connecting the cocking or auxilliary link axis pin to the end of the breech plug. When the breech plug had been charged with a pellet, the plug was moved to the closed position by the action of returning the cocking lever to its locked position under the barrel. A patent covering this modification was granted to Messrs. Taylor and Gardner in 1906.

It was reported in *"The Sporting Goods Review and Gunmaker"* on May 15th, 1906, that an Armour Sergeant Parsons had succeeded in "attaching an air gun to the service rifle thus permitting indoor practice with practically the same weapon as that used in the field". It would appear that Sergeant Parsons was aided and advised in this project, by Mr. Leslie Bown Taylor of Westley Richards as all the development work was carried out at Westley Richards' Bournbrook workshops.

Possibly due to the very high degree of accuracy being achieved with the new fixed barrel BSA air rifle, Sergeant Parsons had the foresight to see its potential as a cheap, military training weapon. Although the air rifle as produced by BSA and Lincoln Jeffries was admirable for teaching the basic principals of rifle shooting, such as correct hold, slight alignment, trigger pressure etc. its use in no way reproduced the handling qualities of the current Long Action Lee-Enfield Territorial Pattern rifle in ·303 calibre and the lighter, shorter, more sporting style air rifles of the period could contribute very little to the teaching of riflemanship to adult servicemen.

Mr. Taylor and Sergeant F. H. Parsons modified an ordinary pattern BSA Air Rifle by fitting it to a Long Lee-Enfield stock and modified fore end so that in profile it resembled the full size territorial service rifle. A longer barrel was fitted to provide the same sight base as the service rifle of 21". An extension was fitted to the rear of the cylinder so that the military style trigger and trigger guard with its removable box magazine could be fitted. The trigger was connected to the sear of the air rifle by a long linking bar. A dummy bolt handle was fastened to the cylinder extension and service pattern sights fixed to the barrel and cylinder completed the modifications (see Plate 44). The adapted air rifle weighed 9¼" lbs., the same weight as its full bore territorial service counterpart. The new rifle was given the long and very descriptive title of "The Westley Richards New Combination Air Gun and Service Rifle".

A patent was applied for which also incorporated the new self-operating breech plug, the patent for which was granted earlier in the year. The application was accepted in November 1906 and given patent number 5496/06. The new Military Air Rifle was briefly mentioned in the *Sporting Goods Review and Gunmaker* of May 1906, where it was reported that the rifle was first produced and tested in February of that year.

Possibly only one, or at the most, two or three models were made by Westley Richards on an experimental basis for submission to the War Office in the hope that the design would be accepted as the basis for an official military training rifle. It has not been possible to confirm any business discussions between Westley Richards and BSA, but it is reasonable to assume that these did take place as by the early part of 1907, BSA had started a limited production run of their own modified version of Westley Richards design which they launched on the Shooting public at Bisley in July, where its introduction prompted the literary rebuke to BSA for claiming the new rifle as a purely BSA innovation, which fact was mentioned earlier in this book.

In the Trade Journal *"Arms and Explosives"*, a short mention was made in the September 1907 issue, that the BSA Military Air Rifle was the result of a complete redesign by BSA of the Westley Richards Patent Military Air Rifle. It was stated that all previous weaknesses had been eliminated by BSA as a result of experience gained after two years of manufacturing their ordinary pattern air rifle. This statement was more than likely made in order to "clear the air" with BSA who, after all, were a major contributor to and advertiser in the journal and must have been very annoyed and embarassed by the critical editorial in the previous month's issue.

BSA had, however, carried out several major improvements to the Westley Richards original concept of the Military air rifle. The trigger mechanism had been simplified by fitting a longer piston rod in the piston and by redesigning the trigger. A flat leaf spring was fitted to provide the heavier trigger pull weight required for service rifle simulation and the trigger release weight was now adjustable by means of an adjusting screw and locking screw. The weight could now be fully adjusted from 2-5 lbs. To facilitate trigger pressure adjustment, the standard pattern Lee-Enfield trigger guard and magazine were replaced by a redesigned trigger guard which was retained at its forward end by a large screw incorporating a standard military sling swivel; a sling eye was also fixed to the barrel forward of the cocking lever catch block. A stronger, much more powerful spring was used which was made for the first time using round section wire and had thirty full coils.

A most important modification was to remove the complicated self-opening and closing breech plug system on the prototype rifle. In theory, this was seen as a major improvement in design, eliminating two operations in loading the air rifle, making the process quicker and simpler. In practice, however, the new device had several faults. It was found that the action of loading the rifle with the cocking or hand lever in the fully open position, was very awkward, particularly when shooting from the prone position which was much favoured by most indoor training ranges. Handling a rifle with the cocking lever in the open position also proved to be very hazardous and had a damaging effect on hands!

The automatic breech plug system also involved the use of several non-standard parts and would mean more complicated stock control and this was to be avoided to reduce production costs.

The BSA Military Pattern Air Rifle was fitted with the same breech plug system as the Improved Model BSA Air Rifle. The cocking lever arrangement was also the same. Standard Ordinary pattern cylinders were used but were marked: The BSA Air Rifle (Military Pattern) The Birmingham Small Arms Company Limited. Sole Manufacturers (see Plate 37), impressed deeply along the top of the cylinder. Serial numbering started at No. 1 and continued to approximately number 150. Rifles within this series of numbers were assembled between February and August 1907, after which date several minor changes occurred.

The marketing behaviour of BSA in relation to this new air rifle development was uncharacteristic being quite unlike their usual forceful and rather showy salesmanship. The new air rifle was only intended for an entirely new and very selective market, namely the British and Colonial Armed Forces. Other than the demonstration of the rifle at the Bisley meeting and the brief announcement to the trade press, no attempt appears to have been made to promote the new model directly to the public. The Bisley meeting was an ideal opportunity to launch the rifle as it was the annual Mecca of expert riflemen from all branches of home and overseas armed forces.

It should be recognised that the rifle was developed solely as a cheap aid to familiarise trainees with usage of the current territorial service rifle and the price of 80/- (£4.00) being asked by BSA, was almost double that of the new Improved Model Air Rifle at 45/- (£2.25). There is no evidence that the Military Pattern Air Rifle was initially sold to the trade, nearly all of the first batch of rifles would have been supplied as free samples to various Government purchasing departments or sold directly to the War Office for assessment as a practical training weapon, by selected regiments and organisations.

In the new advertising booklet published by BSA on 24th August, 1907 entitled "The Improved BSA Air Rifle", no mention or reference was made to the Military Air Rifle, although by that date about 150 had been produced. However, the Company did take a full page advertisement for the Military Air Rifle in the small handbook "The Complete Airgunner" published the same month (see Plate 16).

BSA had conflicting interests in the promotion of the military training air rifle. Earlier in the previous year of 1906, the Company had won a contract from the War Office for the supply of 100,000 .22 Long Rifle Calibre Miniature bolt action training rifles. These were used by all branches of the armed forces and in addition had been supplied in large quantities to Cadet Corps, Boys Clubs, Working Mens Clubs, Public School Cadet Forces and other similar organisations. By August 1907, these miniature rifles were being supplied to the trade and were being eagerly bought by members of the public for use as sporting rifles for small game and vermin shooting. The initial purchase price of 45/- (£2.25) was the same as that for the Improved BSA Air Rifle and was considerably less than a Rook and Rabbit Sporting Rifle supplied by any of the London or Provincial Gunmakers.

Prior to the approval of the BSA .22 Miniature Rifle by the War Office, many serious attempts had been made to provide the forces with an economic method of marksmanship training. Several proposals were accepted. A reasonably successful and popular adaption was the Morris Tube Adaptor. This device comprised of a rifled tube which could be fitted into the bore of a standard .303 calibre service rifle. The breech end of the tube had the same form as the chamber of the rifle and was itself chambered for a diminutive flanged bottle necked cartridge which had a central percussion cap allowing it to be fired by using the standard rifle bolt (see Plate 38). After firing, the cartridge case had to be manually extracted using a special extraction tool. Using this device was slow, cumbersome and quite expensive at £2 16s. 0d. (£2.80) per 1000 rounds; more than the cost of a standard BSA Air Rifle.

Another device, the Kynoch .303 ADAPTOR cartridge, had short lived success in some regiments. This system required no modification in any way of the standard service rifle. The Adaptor had the same shape and form as the .303 Mk. VI service cartridge but was made from steel having a straight, almost parallel, chamber of about .310 calibre.

The big headed, short cartridge had a centre fire percussion cap and was loaded with a lead bullet of about 50 grains weight. On firing, the bullet used the rifling of the service barrel and the complete adaptor could be loaded either singly or from the box magazine in the same way as a service cartridge. Whereas, the Morris Tube device used a standard .297/.230 long or short rook rifle cartridge already commercially available (see Plate 39), the Kynoch .303 Adaptor utilised a unique cartridge which had been specially developed for the purpose.

It is not unreasonable to assume that BSA deliberately under sold the new Military Air Rifle so as not to adversely affect sales of the new .22 Miniature Rifle, which was at that time having a very profitable production run.

All of the cartridge utilising systems of service rifle training including the special miniature rifle, had restrictions on their usage. As well as the already mentioned expense, all were noisy and all required constructed ranges for their safe use. During the winter months, service rifle training virtually stopped and BSA now realised that they could promote the Military Pattern Air Rifle for indoor winter shooting and also for use on school playing fields, sports grounds, village greens etc. requiring a minimal back stop due to the restricted range of the air rifle. Although priced too high for individual purchase, it was considered that the price was not beyond the pockets of groups and organisations.

In their limited advertising, BSA claimed that a Military Air Rifle and 7,000 pellets could be purchased for the same price as 7,000 rounds of .22 ammunition for the Miniature Rifle or 3,000 rounds of Morris Tube ammunition (see Plate 16). They now stated that the Military Air Rifle was used by many regiments, including the Royal Horse Guards. The Local Birmingham Regiment, the 1st V.B. Royal Warwickshire Regiment and The Central London Rangers. Several Public and Grammar School Cadet Forces were also equipped with the new air rifle. Streatham Grammar School Cadet Force boasted at least three as photographs of the cadets using the new rifles were included in the book ''The Complete Airgunner''.

PLATE 62 *(G. Kerry)*
A BSA Air Rifle Improved Model 'D' .22 Calibre Sporting Rifle
in its original wooden carrying box.

128

THE "LINCOLN"
PATENT AIR-RIFLE, (Improved Pattern)

With Fixed Barrel and Under Cocking Lever (Lincoln Jeffries Patent)

THE NEW ADJUSTABLE BREECH PLUG.

This ingenious addition to the Lincoln Rifle permits of the Rifle barrel being quickly examined, which cannot be done where the breech plug is held in position with screws and washers. It will not get loose by wear, the spring always keeping the breech plug firmly on its bearings.

Unscrew the breech plug thumb screw with the finger and thumb, remove the breech plug, when the inside of the barrel can be examined and any obstruction removed.

Can be fitted to all the Lincoln Patent Rifles at nominal cost, 1 6 You can fix it yourself without sending your Rifle. When ordering be sure and ask for the up-to-date pattern Rifle with the quickly adjustable breech plug

The only interchangeable Air Rifle manufactured :

—— Price, 45/- and 50/- each. ——

21

Showing breech plug and thumb screw in position ready for use.

PLATE 63 *(G. Kerry)*
Details of the New Adjustable Breech Plug of 1906.

129

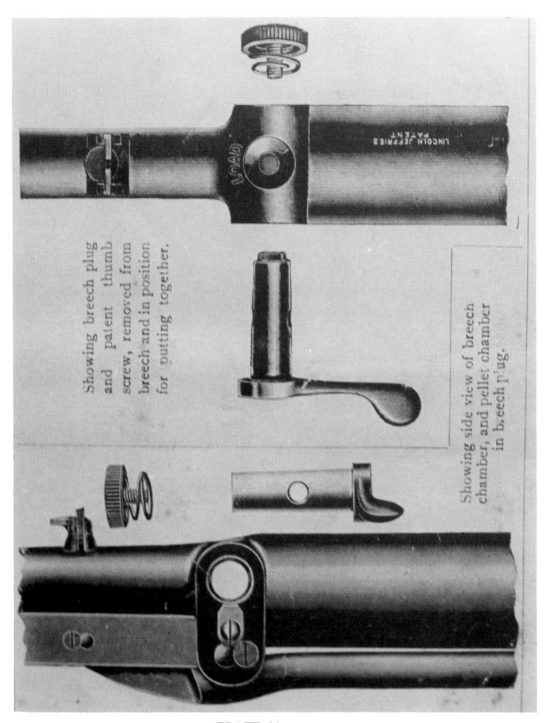

Showing breech plug and patent thumb screw, removed from breech and in position for putting together.

Showing side view of breech chamber, and pellet chamber in breech plug.

PLATE 64 *(G. Kerry)*
Lincoln Jeffries New Adjustable Breech Plug Modification described in a 1906 Catalogue.

Chapter 19

THE SECOND batch of rifles was approximately 130 in quantity the serial numbers running consecutive with the first batch numbering approximately 151-280. Manufacture commenced in early 1908 and was sporadic up to mid 1911. Although batches of a hundred or so components were made for the Military Pattern Air Rifle, mainly Barrel & Cylinder assemblies, Trigger Guards, Back Blocks, Fore Ends etc., rifles were not assembled and put into stock as were standard production models. It is quite evident from examination of existing specimens that assembly of this model was to order and as trigger blocks were numbered during manufacture and then put into store until required, the actual component structure of this model did not follow a logical sequence as will be discussed later.

This second batch of rifles was assembled using major components contemporary with models of current production. Most had cocking hand levers with the strengthening fillets introduced by BSA in their ordinary and light pattern models in August 1907 (see Plate 40). Some of the batch utilized the improved pattern of breech plug with the small central plug on the retaining plate and the indexing spring and plunger. However, some rifles were assembled with the older type of breech plug having the large central peg on the retaining plate and the heavy compensating spring. Some rifles from this batch assembled near the end of the run in 1911, were fitted with the improved Mark II cocking hand lever catch with the side button release introduced to BSA production models in mid 1911 (see Plates 41 and 42). These rifles were not necessarily assembled in serial number sequence and some low numbered models, for example, No. 137, was fitted with a 1911 pattern side button hand lever release catch and a much earlier pattern breech plug of 1907 pattern. During the four years of this second batch production, a change took place in the identification marking on the cylinder of the rifle. Models assembled early in the period were inscribed "The BSA Air Rifle Military Patt. The Birmingham Small Arms Company Limited. Sole Manufacturers", on the cylinder itself with the back block left plain. Later in the batch, the back or trigger block itself was engraved with the words "BSA Military Air Rifle" (see Plate 43). Several styles of stock were fitted. Some early rifles had standard Government issue stocks with brass heel plates, other had poorer quality, probably Government reject, stocks fitted with sheet steel heel plates. The latter are more usually found by collectors.

The last or third batch of Military Air Rifles was manufactured from mid 1911 up to the outbreak of the Great War in late 1914. Serial numbers ran from 280 up to 400, or possibly slightly higher, although no number higher than 392 has been identified. All the known examples of this last batch were fitted with side button release hand cocking levers and this batch was made in two calibres of .177 or .22, the latter being predominent. During the period of production of this batch, it was recognised that the .22 calibre Improved Model 'D' sporting rifle was a very effective target weapon at ranges of up to 50 yards and to encourage long range outdoor target shooting, the BSA Military Air Rifle was produced in this heavier calibre also.

As already mentioned, assembly of the Military Pattern Air Rifles was to individual order using parts already manufactured for this specific model or parts taken from current production. It will be found by collectors that a great many anomalies exist in the Military Pattern range. The actual rifle produced depended very much on the availability of parts at the time of assembly. Due to this practice, some very unusual and quite incorrectly suspect models, were produced, all of which are genuine but component parts will be found to be very inconsistent with contemporary air rifle production.

In an endeavour to provide a comprehensive range of training rifles, BSA listed in 1911, a second version of the Military Pattern Air Rifle to compare with the Short Magazine Lee Enfield Military Service rifle which at that time had been issued to the armed forces in 1902. The now obsolete Lee Metford rifle issued in 1888 and the Long Lee Enfield issued in 1985 were now in use by the Territorial and Cadet Forces.

In the BSA advertising booklet of 1911, the short version of the Military Pattern Air Rifle was offered at the unbelievably high price of 120/- (£6.00) (see Plate 45). The printed specification gave the short model rifle an overall length of 44½″ as compared with the Long version of 49½″. A sight base of 19½″ compared with 21″ for the Long Pattern and a reduced weight of 8 lbs. 11 ozs., 9 ozs. higher than the long pattern weight of 9 lbs. 4 ozs.

No specimen of the Short Pattern Military Air Rifle has been examined to date. The author has carried out extensive investigations into this matter and is of the opinion that although advertised, the short pattern was never actually manufactured as a production model. One or two samples may have been made experimentally, but no evidence exists that the short pattern was produced commercially. To support this assumption, BSA in their advertising of August 1913, mention only the long Magazine Lee Enfield and the long version of the Military Pattern Air Rifle. No mention at all is made of the Short Magazine Lee Enfield model, although at that time the factory had produced many thousands of Short Magazine Lee Enfield rifles for the War Office under contract (see Plate 46).

The Short Magazine Lee Enfield Rifle was issued to serving regiments of the British Army only. Volunteer, Territorial regiments and Cadet Corps all still used the now obsolete Long Lee Enfield Service rifle so they would have had no interest in an air rifle version of the latest military rifle to which they would not have had access. An example of the BSA Military Pattern Air Rifle Short version has yet to be authenticated.

A total of just over 400 BSA Military Pattern Air Rifles were produced between 1907 and 1914. All were long versions resembling the Long Lee Enfield Territorial Rifle of the period (see Plate 40). Approximately 150 were fitted with early pattern hand cocking levers with no strenghtening fillets; all these were in .177 calibre. Approximately 130 were fitted with second pattern hand cocking levers with strengthening fillets, again most of these were in .177 calibre only with a small number in .22 calibre. The final 120 were mostly fitted with hand cocking levers incorporating the patented side button release catch. The majority of this final batch were made in .22 calibre with only a very small quantity being made in .177 calibre.

Collectors and enthusiasts who have examined and fired any of the Military Pattern Air Rifles cannot but admire the efficient performance and remarkable accuracy of these fascinating variations of the fixed barrel air rifle system. Many modern mass produced air rifles cannot hold a candle to these giant rifles as regards handling qualities and long range accuracy. In view of these last mentioned qualities, it is surprising to learn that the BSA Military Pattern Air Rifle was never officially approved for military use by the War Office or any other Government Department. The only spring operated air rifle so approved was the Webley & Scott Service Mark II Air Rifle approval of which was granted of course, after the Great War.

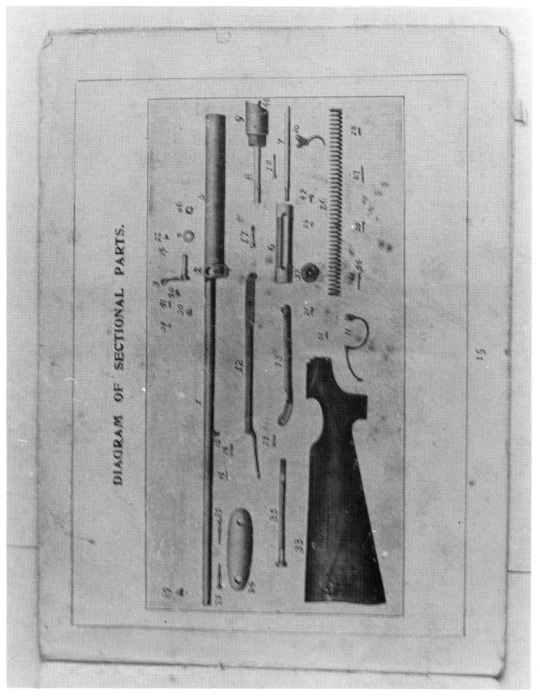

PLATE 65 *(G. Kerry)*
A page from Lincoln Jeffries Catalogue of 1906, showing a complete breakdown of the
Lincoln Air Rifle.

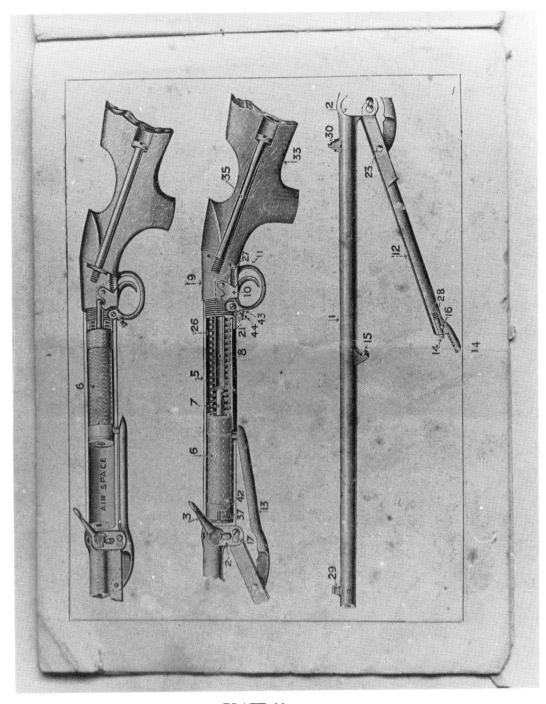

PLATE 66 *(G. Kerry)*
Details of the mechanism of the Lincoln Air Rifle showing the BSA Patent Breech Plug Fastening.
Lincoln Jeffries Catalogue of 1906.

135

PLATE 67 *(Mr. Lincoln Jeffries)*
The headstone of the grave of George Lincoln Jeffries in Warstone Lane Cemetery, Birmingham.

Chapter 20

THE WAR OFFICE did, however, approve an adaption of the Standard, or Ordinary Pattern, of the BSA Air Rifle so that it could be used to teach correct gun laying and firing of both naval and field artillery.

In September 1913, the new "Gun Laying Teacher" as the new modification was called, was mentioned in the Trade Journal of the period. Although a few models were completed and sent to various Government Departments for assessment, in late 1913, the Gun Laying Teacher did not go into full production until June 1915 when 212 were produced and supplied to the Admiralty and the Royal Field Artillery where the Teacher was fitted to both Light and Heavy field guns (see Plate 47).

All the Teachers were supplied in .177 bore only. The modified air rifle was fitted to two stout brackets which enabled it to be fitted directly on the barrel of the field piece. Both horizontal and vertical adjustment was provided in order that the air rifle could be zeroed to the axis of the barrel of the larger gun. When correctly zeroed the Teacher was firmly fixed to the larger gunbarrel and when the field gun was elevated to suit an increased range, the Laying Teacher, by means of an elevating screw (which was marked to agree precisely with the range marking of the sight of the field gun as shown by the appropriate range table) could be depressed through a corresponding number of degrees (see Plate 48).

Practice with this new device could be carried out at ranges of up to 20 yards, so a large drill hall or other building could be used. The target used was a six foot square steel plate ⅜″ thick which was coated with non-drying grey or white paint to show up the impact of the lead pellet. Scale models of buildings, batteries, trenches, troop formations etc. were cut out of coloured paper and stuck on to the target plate. All the correct and proper principles could be followed using this new device, even to the extent of having to use field glasses to record correct or incorrect pellet strikes.

The Gun Laying Teacher was last delivered to the armed forces in January 1916, but so successful was the air rifle in teaching the rudiments of correct gun laying and firing that during the Second World War an improved pattern of Gun Laying Teacher which could be actually fitted inside the barrel of a two pounder gun was used to train tank crews throughout the period of the war. These gun laying trainers were still in use in 1953 by the Armed Forces of New Zealand and were used to train crews for the Valentine Tank.

The actual initial design of the Gun Laying Teacher was approved by the War Office in Mid 1911 and plans were drawn up together with detailed specifications at that time. As many standard components as possible were used but certain parts had to be adapted specially for this new air rifle modification. The lever on the breech plug was redesigned so that it could be easily and positively operated from the rear position. The trigger was also redesigned so that it would be operated by an electrical solenoid which was fitted as standard to all Admiralty Pattern Gun Laying Teachers (see Plate 70). The trigger of the Land Pattern Gun Laying Teacher was either bent foreward or drilled with a hole to enable firing to be carried out by using a lanyard. Although the piston and cylinder of the Gun Laying Teacher was of standard dimensions the wall thickness of the cylinder was considerably increased to withstand the extra wear on this component produced by the cocking slide.

All Air Rifles manufactured as Gun Laying Teachers were tested at Enfield Lock to check that they met the stringent accuracy specification. When fixed to a rigid table or stand, 10 shots fired at 10 yards all had to group in a circle of $\frac{3}{8}''$. Adder Brand Pellets were used for this accuracy test. All approved rifles were marked with a Broad Arrow above the view mark and the letter 'N' on the barrel in front of the loading hole.

PLATE 68 *(Mr. Lincoln Jeffries)*
Mr. George Lincoln Jeffries (centre) outside 121 Steelhouse Lane, Birmingham. On the left is
Mr. H. Sprawson, an airgunner who scored 108 consecutive bulls with the Lincoln Air Rifle.
Circa 1906.

PLATE 69 *(G. Kerry)*
Cylinder markings on Admiralty Pattern Gun Laying Teacher.

PLATE 70 *(G. Kerry)*
The Admiralty Pattern Gun Laying Teacher fixed on its approved Holder or Mounting Carriage.

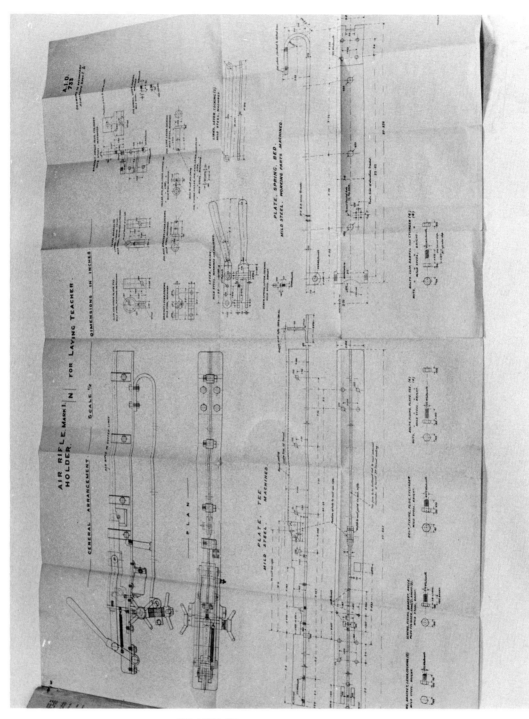

PLATE 71 *(Pattern Room Enfield Lock)*
Government drawing of the Holder for the Gun Laying Teacher Air Rifle.

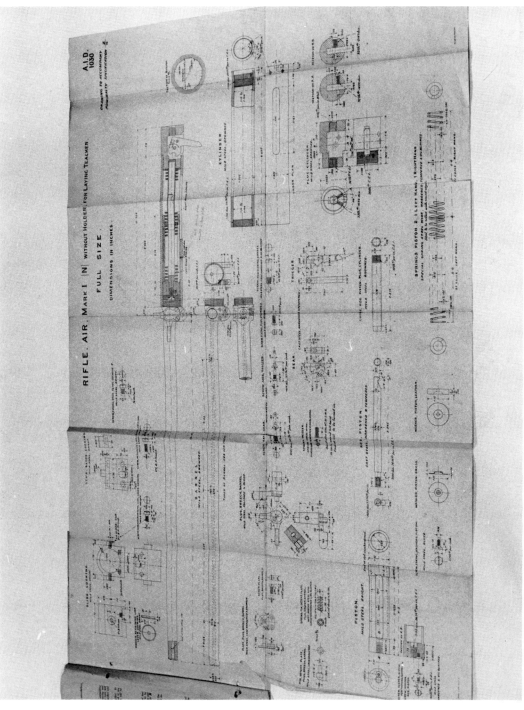

PLATE 72 *(Pattern Room Enfield Lock)*
Government drawing of the Gun Laying Teacher Air Rifle.

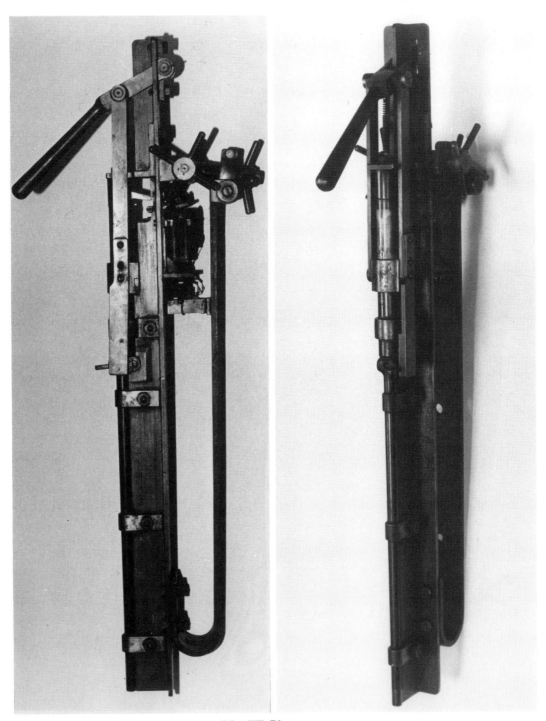

PLATE 73 *(G. Kerry)*
Two views of the Admiralty Gun Laying Teacher fixed in its Holder. Note Solenoid Release.

144

INDEX OF SERIAL NUMBERS

As a result of information which has come to light during the researches for this book and with reference to hand written warehouse records very kindly made available by BSA Guns Ltd., it has been possible to prepare a tabulation of series of serial numbers with their relation to manufacturing and despatch dates.

Attempts have been made to relate serial numbers with manufacturing dates by other serious researchers some years ago. Mr. D. H. Commins and Mr. P. J. Coleman both published information which has been invaluable to collectors and enthusiasts alike. Unfortunately, due mainly to the limited material available at that time, some of the published material is technically and chronologically incorrect and its acceptance as fact has resulted in misunderstanding and incorrect identification of some models. This misinformation has very recently been compounded by the reproduction of the original material as irrefutable fact, the perpetrators not even bothering to check the authenticity of the information which they are reprinting.

The purpose of the following tabulation is to provide for collectors and enthusiasts information of an updated nature so that more positive identification can be made. The Author does not in any way wish to challenge or denegrate the initial material published by Mr. Commins or Mr. Coleman as indeed it was their splendid initial researches which helped to inspire his own efforts into deeper and more detailed investigation of the fascinating history of the development of the BSA Air Rifle.

Early serial numbers are classified in batches relating to actual production quantities of the period. As batches became larger in quantity, the serial numbers have been grouped into smaller batches to isolate more precise changes. Reference to existing factory records have indicated that a convenient component manufacturing and weapon assembly batch size was 500 units and this practice has been followed in the index.

Manufacturing dates have been calculated as accurately as possible using surviving records, Trade Publications, advertising information and examination of rifles in various collections. Account has also been taken of manufacturing capacity in the factory at that period, particularly in respect to other, usually military, contracts in hand.

Despatch dates will be seen to cover quite extended periods of several years and in some cases will be considerably after a manufacturing period. These despatch dates are accurate having been compiled from the, at times, seemingly unending study and analysis of hand written, often very badly, warehouse records which have managed to survive two World Wars, five major moves and a quite unprovoked attack on the factory by Herman Goering on August 26, 1940. This research involved the study of over 400 closely hand written pages from record ledgers so any mistakes discovered by a future enthusiast are purely unintentional (see Plate 49).

In order to provide as comprehensive an index as possible, notes relevant to manufacturing, despatch dates or model types have been included and in instances of extended despatch periods, dates of despatch of the majority of the batch have been indicated.

It is recommended that the index is used in conjunction with the main text and is not used purely in isolation for identification purposes.

Serial Numbers	Period of Manufacture	Period of Despatch	Notes
1-129	1901-04	1901-04	First experimental Lincoln Air Rifles H Prefix to Serial Numbers.
103-1129	Mid. 1905	Mid. 1905	First Lincoln Rifles made by BSA.
1130-2129	Sept./Dec. 1905	Last Quarter 1905	First BSA Air Rifles (Lincoln Jeffries Patent).
2130-2729	Jan./Sept. 1906	Jan./Sept. 1906	Second batch Lincolns. First Ladies Pattern.
2730-3229	Jan./Feb. 1906	Jan./April 1906	Second batch BSA. 1 Desp. June 1907. 1—April 1912.
3230-3529	Feb. 1906	Feb./Sept. 1906	Second batch BSA. All Standard Pattern .177.
3530-4029	Feb./March 1906	Feb. 1906/Aug. 1907	Second batch BSA. First Cast Improved Trigger Guard, with small diameter Rear Locating Peg.
4030-4529	March/April 1906	March/Sept. 1906	Second Batch BSA. All Standard Pattern .177.
4530-4829	April/May 1906	April/Sept. 1906	Last of second batch BSA. All Standard Pattern.
4830-5329	Jan./March 1906	Jan./July 1906	Third batch Lincolns. Standard & Ladies Pattern.
5330-5829	June/July 1906	June/Sept. 1906	Third batch Lincolns Standard & Ladies Pattern.
5830-6329	May/July 1906	May 1906/March 1907	Third batch BSA. All Standard Pattern.
6330-6829	July/Aug. 1906	July/Sept. 1906	Third batch BSA. All Standard Pattern.
6380-7329	Aug./Oct. 1906	Aug 1906/April 1908	Third batch BSA. All Standard Pattern.
7330-7829	Sept./Oct. 1906	Sept. 1906/May 1908	Finish of third batch BSA. All Standard Pattern.
7830-8329	Sept./Oct. 1906	Sept./Nov. 1906	Fourth batch Lincolns. Variety of Breech Plugs.
8330-8829	Oct./Nov. 1906	Oct./Nov. 1906	Fourth batch Lincolns. Variety of Breech Plugs.
8830-9329	Oct./Nov. 1906	Oct. 1906/Oct. 1908	Fourth batch BSA. Standard & Light Patterns.
9330-9829	Nov./Dec. 1906	Nov. 1906/Nov. 1908	Fourth batch BSA. Standard Patterns.
9830-10229	Nov./Dec. 1906	Nov. 1906/Oct. 1908	Fourth batch BSA. Standard & Light Patterns. First Improved Models but not marked as such.
10230-10409	Nov./Dec. 1906	Nov./Dec. 1906	Fifth batch Lincolns. Standard & Ladies Pattern.
10410-10509	May 1908	May/Nov. 1908	Fifth batch Lincolns. Standard Possibly .250" Cal.
10510-10729	Dec. 1906/Jan. 1907	Dec. 1906/Nov. 1907	Fifth batch Lincolns Standard Pattern.
10730-11229	Jan./Feb. 1907	Jan. 1907/July 1908	Fifth batch Lincolns Standard & Ladies Pattern.
11230-11729	Dec. 1906/Jan. 1907	Dec. 1906/Nov. 1908	Fifth batch BSA. Standard & Light Pattern. Improved Models.
11730-12229	Dec. 1906/Jan. 1907	Dec. 1906/April 1908	Fifth batch BSA. Standard & Light Pattern. 1 Desp. July 1913. Improved Models.
12230-12729	Jan./Feb. 1907	Jan./Nov. 1907	Fifth batch BSA Standard & Light Pattern. Improved Models.
12730-13229	Jan./March 1907	Jan. 1907/May 1908	Fifth batch BSA Standard & Light Pattern. Improved Models.
13230-13729	June/Oct. 1907	June 1907/Sept. 1908	Sixth batch Lincolns Standard & Ladies Pattern.
13730-14229	Sept. 1907/Jan. 1908	Sept. 1907/Sept. 1908	Sixth batch Lincolns Standard & Ladies Pattern. First production of .22 calibre rifles short cylinder.

Serial Numbers	Period of Manufacture	Period of Despatch	Notes
14230-14729	Feb./March 1907	Feb. 1907/Nov. 1908	Sixth batch BSA. Standard & Light Pattern. First Improved Model 'B'.
14730-15229	May/June 1907	May 1907/Nov. 1908	Sixth batch BSA. Standard & Light Pattern. Improved Model 'B'.
15230-15729	May/July 1907	May 1907/Oct. 1908	Sixth batch BSA Standard & Light Pattern. Improved Model 'B'.
15730-16229	May/July 1907	May 1907/Oct. 1908	Sixth batch BSA Standard & Light Pattern. Improved Model 'B'.
16230-16729	June/Nov. 1907	June 1907/Nov. 1908	Sixth batch BSA All Standard Pattern. Improved Model 'B'.
16730-17229	July/Sept. 1907	July 1907/Feb. 1908	Sixth batch BSA mostly Standard with few Light Pattern. Improved Model 'B'.
17230-17729	Aug./Oct. 1907	Aug. 1907/Jan. 1908	BSA Improved Model 'B' Standard & Light Pattern. 1 Despatched May 1912.
17730-18229	Aug. Nov. 1907	Aug. 1907/Nov. 1908	BSA Improved Model 'B' Standard & Light Pattern.
18230-18729	Sept. 1907/Jan. 1908	Sept. 1907/Nov. 1908	BSA Improved Model 'B' Standard & Light Pattern. First Improved Model 'D'.
18730-19229	Nov. 1907/Feb. 1908	Nov. 1907/Sept. 1908	Improved Model 'D' in .177 and .22 standard length cylinder.
19230-19729	Dec. 1907/March 1908	Dec. 1907/April 1909	Imp. Mod. 'D' .177 Standard & Light Pattern. 2 Rifles despatched Feb. 1912.
19730-20229	March/July 1908	March 1908/Aug. 1909	Imp. Mod. 'D' Standard Pattern .177, .22 & .250″ Light Pattern.
20230-20729	April/July 1908	April 1908/Oct. 1909	Imp. Mod. 'D' Standard & Light .177, .22, .250″.
20730-21229	July/Dec. 1908	July 1908/May 1909	Imp. Mod. 'D' Standard & Light .177, .22. First Long Cylinder .250″.
21230-21729	Sept./Dec. 1908	Sept. 1908/Sept. 1914	BSA Long Cylinder .22 Standard & Light Pattern .177, Long Cylinder .250″. Improved Model 'D'.
21730-22229	July 1908/Jan. 1909	July 1908/April 1910	BSA Standard & Light Pattern .177, Long Cylinder .22, Long Cylinder 250″. Improved Model 'D'.
22230-22529	Aug. 1908/Jan. 1909	Aug. 1908/Oct. 1909	BSA Standard & Light Pattern .177. Long Cylinder .22 & .250. One .250″ Despatched 1914. Sept. All BSA Rifles were Improved Model 'D' from hereon.
22530-23029	March 1908/Nov. 1909	March 1908/April 1910	All Lincoln Models Standard .177 & .22 and few .250″ Calibre and several Ladies Pattern. Seventh batch.
23030-23529	Oct. 1908/Aug. 1913	Oct. 1908/Nov. 1913	All Lincoln Models All Calibres and sizes. 8 Imp. Mod. 'D' BSA.
23530-24029	Nov. 1908/April 1909	Nov. 1908/Aug. 1911	BSA Standard, Light Pattern .177 & .22. Few .250″ Cal.
24030-24529	Jan./April 1909	Jan. 1909/July 1913	BSA Standard, Light Pattern .177 & .22. Several .250″ Cal.
24530-25029	Jan./May 1909	Jan. 1909/Jan. 1912	BSA Standard .177, & .22. 200 Light Pattern.
25030-25529	March/Sept. 1909	March 1909/Oct. 1912	BSA Standard .177 & .22. 80 Light Pattern. Few .250″.
24430-26029	April/Sept. 1909	April 1909/Jan. 1912	BSA Standard .177 & .22.

Serial Numbers	Period of Manufacture	Period of Despatch	Notes
26030-26529	April/Sept. 1909	April/Nov. 1909	BSA Standard .177 & .22 & 100 Light Pattern.
26530-27029	Sept. 1909/July 1910	Sept. 1909/Nov. 1911	BSA Standard .177 & .22.
27030-27529	July/Sept. 1909	July 1909/Aug. 1912	BSA Standard .177 & .22. Few Light Patterns including .250″ Stds. exported to New Zealand.
27530-28029	Sept. 1909/Jan. 1910	Sept. 1909/Nov. 1911	BSA Standard .177 & .22 including .250″ exported to New Zealand.
28030-28529	Oct. 1909/Jan. 1910	Oct. 1909/Oct. 1910	BSA Standard .177 & .22. 100 Light Patterns.
28530-29029	Sept. 1909/April 1910	Sept. 1909/Aug. 1910	BSA Standard .177 & .22. Few Light Patterns. First Junior Rifle.
29030-29529	Dec. 1909/April 1910	Dec. 1909/Sept. 1912	BSA Standard .177 & .22 Light Pattern. 13 Junior Pattern Rifles.
29530-30029	Jan./July 1910	Jan. 1910/Jan. 1911	BSA Standard .177 & .22 Light Pattern & Junior Pattern.
30030-30529	Feb./Oct. 1910	Feb. 1910/May 1911	BSA Standard .177 & .22 Light Pattern. Large Quantity of Junior Pattern.
30530-31029	April/Oct. 1910	April 1910/Nov. 1912	BSA Standard .177 & .22. Light & Junior Pattern.
31030-31529	Jan./Oct. 1910	Jan. 1910/Feb. 1911	BSA Standard .177 & .22.
31530-32029	March/Nov. 1910	March 1910/1912	BSA Standard .177 & .22.
32030-32529	Oct. 1910/Feb. 1911	Oct. 1910/Dec. 1911	BSA Standard .177 & .22.
32530-33029	May/Oct. 1910	May 1910/July 1912	BSA Standard .177 & .22 including 30 Light Patterns.
33030-33529	May/Oct. 1910	May/Nov. 1910	BSA Standard .177 & .22. Few Light Patterns, 26 Junior, 1 Standard. Despatched 1914, 2—1916.
33530-34029	June/Nov. 1910	June 1910/Feb. 1911	Mostly Light & Junior with few Standard .177 or .22.
34030-34529	Aug. 1910/March 1911	Aug. 1910/March 1911	All BSA Light and Junior Pattern.
34530-35029	Oct. 1910/March 1911	Oct. 1910/March 1911	Mostly Light & Junior Pattern with few Standard .177 & .22.
35030-35529	Aug. 1910/July 1912	Aug. 1910/March 1913	Last batch of Lincoln Air Rifles. Mostly Standard .177 & .22, few Ladies Pattern. Numbers 35312-35529 not issued.
35530-36029	Nov. 1910/March 1911	Nov. 1910/April 1911	Mostly Light & Standard .177. Few .22 and few Junior Pattern.
36030-36529	Nov. 1910/Jan. 1911	Nov. 1910/April 1911	Mostly Light & Standard Pattern .177, few .22 and few Junior. Majority despatched Dec. 1910.
36530-37029	Nov. 1910/Feb. 1911	Nov. 1910/April 1911	Mixture of Light, Standard, Junior and .22. Majority despatched Dec. 1910.
37030-37529	Dec. 1910/March 1911	Dec. 1910/Feb. 1912	Mixture of Light, Standard, Junior and .22. Majority despatched Jan. & Feb. 1911.
37530-38029	Jan./April 1911	Jan. 1911/June 1918	Standard & Light Pattern with few Junior. Majority despatched Spring 1911. Remainder 1913, 1914, 1915 and 1918.
38030-38529	Feb./April 1911	Feb. 1911/Oct. 1913	All Standard .177 & .22. Majority despatched Spring 1911.
38530-39029	Feb./April 1911	Feb./Dec. 1911	Mixture of Standard Light Junior & .22. Majority despatched April-June 1911.
39030-39529	March/April 1911	March/Dec. 1911	Mostly Standard .177 & .22. Few Light & several Junior. Most despatched Summer 1911.

Serial Numbers	Period of Manufacture	Period of Despatch	Notes
39530-40029	Feb./May 1911	Feb./Aug. 1911	All Standard .177 & .22. Most despatched April-May 1911.
40030-40529	April/July 1911	April 1911/Aug. 1914	Standard .177 & .22. Most despatched June-Sept. 1911.
40530-41029	March/May 1911	March 1911/Jan. 1912	Mostly Standard .177 & .22. Few Light and Junior Pattern. Most despatched May 1911.
41030-41529	April/June 1911	April/Sept. 1911	Equal quantities Standard & Light .177. Few .22 & 7 Juniors. Most despatched May-July 1911.
41530-42029	May/July 1911	May 1911/Jan. 1914	Mostly Standard .177 & .22. Few Light Patterns. Most despatched Summer 1911.
42030-42529	May/July 1911	May 1911/Oct. 1916	Mixture of Light & few Juniors. Very few Standards. Most despatched Mid. 1911.
42530-43029	May/Aug. 1911	May 1911/Nov. 1916	Mixture of Standard, Light and 33 Junior. Most despatched July—August 1911.
43030-43529	July/Aug. 1911	July 1911/Nov. 1916	Mixture Standard .177 & .22 Light and Junior. Majority despatched July-Aug. 1911.
43530-44029	July/Aug. 1911	July 1911/July 1914	Majority Light with some Standards and few Juniors. Most despatches July 1911.
44030-44529	July/Sept. 1911	July 1911/Dec. 1914	Majority Light with some Standards and few Juniors. Most despatches July-Aug. 1911.
44530-45029	Aug./Oct. 1911	Aug. 1911/Feb. 1914	Mixture of Standard, Light .177 & .22. 1 Junior. Most despatches Sept.-Oct. 1911.
45030-45529	Sept. 1911/Jan. 1912	Sept. 1911/Nov. 1914	Mostly Light Pattern. Few Standard .177 & .22. Most despatches end 1911.
45530-46029	Sept. 1911/Feb. 1912	Sept. 1911/April 1915	Mostly Light with few Standard. 15 Juniors, most despatches Jan. 1912.
46030-46529	Oct. 1911/Jan. 1912	Oct. 1911/May 1915	Mostly Light with few Standard. Few Juniors. Most despatches Jan. 1912.
46530-47029	Nov. 1911/Feb. 1912	Nov. 1911/Sept. 1912	Mixture Standard .177 & .22 Light & Junior.
47030-47529	Dec. 1911/Feb. 1912	Dec. 1911/Oct. 1913	All Standard .177 & .22. First recorded side button catch. Majority despatched Jan.-Feb. 1912.
47530-48029	Jan./April 1912	Jan. 1912/May 1914	Mostly Standard .177 & .22. Few Light Patterns. Most despatched Spring 1912.
48030-48529	Jan./April 1912	Jan. 1912/Oct. 1914	All Standard .177 or .22. Most .22 with Side Button Catches.
48530-49029	Aug. 1911/Feb. 1912	Aug. 1911/July 1912	All Standard .177 & .22. Most .22 with Side Button Catches.
49030-49529	Sept. 1911/April 1912	Sept. 1911/June 1913	All Standard .177 & .22. Most despatches Winter 1911-12.
49530-50029	Dec. 1911/April 1912	Dec. 1911/Oct. 1914	All Standard .177 & .22. Most despatches Mid. 1912.
50030-50529	March/Sept. 1912	March 1912/Jan. 1913	All Standard .177 & .22. Most despatched April-Sept. 1912.
50530-51029	July/Sept. 1912	July 1912/July 1913	All Standard .177 & .22. Most despatches Sept.-Oct. 1912.
51030-51329	Sept./Dec. 1912	Sept. 1912/Dec. 1915	Most Standard .177 & .22. 1 Light Pattern. Numbers 51172-51210 not issued. Most despatches Winter 1912-13.

Serial Numbers	Period of Manufacture	Period of Despatch	Notes
51530-52029	Feb./April 1913	Feb. 1913/April 1916	All Standard .177 & .22. Most despatches March & April 1913. Introduction of Double Sear. Start of 'S' Prefix numbers.
52030-52529	March/July 1913	March/Sept. 1913	All Standard .177 & .22. Most with 'S' Prefixes.
52530-53029	Feb./April 1912	Feb. 1912/Oct. 1914	All Standard .177 & .22. Most despatches Mid. 1912.
53030-53529	March/May 1912	March 1912/June 1915	.177 and .22 Standards with 100 Light Patterns. Most despatches Spring 1912.
53530-54029	March/April 1912	March 1912/March 1914	410 Light Pattern. 2 Juniors. Remainder Standard. Most despatches March-April 1912.
54030-54529	March/April 1912	March 1912/Nov. 1914	Mostly Light Pattern. 14 Junior. 55 Numbers not issued.
54530-55029	April/May 1912	April 1912/Oct. 1914	Mostly Light Pattern. 12 Junior. Some Standard. 62 numbers not issued.
55030-55529	April/June 1912	April 1912/Nov. 1914	Mostly Light Pattern. 33 Junior. Remainder Standard. Most despatches May 1912.
55530-56029	Jan. 1911/March 1912	Feb. 1911/Nov. 1912	Mostly Standard. 2 Light Pattern. Most despatches Mid. 1912.
65030-56529	Feb./May 1912	Feb. 1912/April 1914	Mostly Light with 65 Juniors. Remainder Standards. Most despatches Mid. 1912.
56530-57029	May/June 1912	May/Dec. 1912	Mixture of Standard .177 & .22 Light and Junior Models. Most despatches June 1912.
57030-57529	May/Sept. 1912	May/Dec. 1912	Standard .177 & .22 Light Pattern. Few Juniors. 65 Numbers not issued.
57530-58029	may/July 1912	June/Nov. 1912	Mostly Light Pattern with few Standards and few Junior. Most despatches June-July 1912.
58030-58529	June/Nov. 1912	June 1912/Nov. 1914	Mixed Standard and Light Pattern with few Juniors. 173 Numbers not issued.
58530-59029	June/Nov. 1912	June 1912/Jan. 1913	Mostly Standard Pattern .177 & .22. 1 Light Pattern. 92 Numbers not issued.
59030-59529	July/Nov. 1912	July 1912/Nov. 1914	Mixed Standard. Light & Junior Patterns. 340 Numbers not issued.
59530-60029	July/Oct. 1912	July 1912/Feb. 1915	Standard & Light Patterns. 4 Juniors. 240 Numbers not issued.
60030-60529	July/Nov. 1912	July 1912/Oct. 1913	Mostly Standard .177 & .22 with few Light Pattern. 101 Numbers not issued.
60530-61029	Aug./Sept. 1912	Aug. 1912/Jan. 1913	Mostly Light Patterns with few Standard and 6 Junior. 45 Numbers not issued.
61030-61529	Aug./Sept. 1912	Aug. 1912/Oct. 1914	Mostly Light with few Standard Pattern and few Junior. 10 Numbers not issued.
62030-62529	Sept. 1912/Dec. 1913	Sept. 1912/Nov. 1914	Mostly Light with very few Standard Patterns. Despatches through 1912-13 and 1914.
62530-63029	Sept. 1912/Dec. 1913	Sept. 1912/March 1915	Light Patterns with few Standards in .177 and .22. Despatches from 1912-15.
63030-63529	Nov. 1912/Nov. 1914	Nov. 12/Nov. 1914	Equal Light & Standard Patterns. 14 Numbers not issued. Despatches throughout 1912-13-14.
63530-64029	Oct. 1912/Nov. 1914	Oct. 1912/Nov. 1914	Majority Light Patterns with few Standards. Despatches throughout 1912-13-14.
64030-64529	Nov. 1912/Nov. 1914	Nov. 1912/Nov. 1914	Mostly Light with very few Standard Patterns. Despatches throughout 1912-13-14.

Serial Numbers	Period of Manufacture	Period of Despatch	Notes
64530-65029	Nov. 1912/Nov. 1914	Nov. 1912/Dec. 1916	Mostly Light Patterns. 80 Standards. 3 Junior with Side Button Cocking Levers. Despatches throughout 1912-13-14-15 into end of 1916. Most Juniors had Side Button Cocking Levers from hereon.
65030-65529	Dec. 1912/Nov. 1914	Dec. 1912/Jan. 1915	Standard and Light Pattern .177, few .22 & First Juvenile. Most despatches Jan. 1913-Nov. 1914.
65530-66029	Nov. 1912/Nov. 1913	Nov. 1912/Nov. 1913	Mostly Juvenile and Junior Pattern with few Light and Standard Patterns.
66030-66525	Feb. 1913/Feb. 1914	Feb. 1913/Feb. 1915	Mostly Standard Patterns .177 & .22. 200 Light Patterns, 1 Junior. Most despatches 1913 and 1914.
66530-67029	Jan. 1913/Dec. 1914	Jan. 1913/March 1917	Mostly Standard Patterns .177 & .22. 110 Light Patterns. Most despatches Spring 1913.
67030-67529	Feb./June 1913	Feb. 1913/May 1915	All Standard .177 & .22. Most despatches Spring & Summer 1913.
67530-68029	March/Dec. 1913	March 1913/July 1914	Mostly Standard Pattern .177 & .22. Few Light Pattern. Most despatches Mid. 1913.
68030-68529	June 1913/Feb. 1914	June 1913/May 1914	All Standard Pattern .177 & .22.
68530-69029	June 1913/Dec. 1914	June 1913/Sept. 1915	Mostly Standard Pattern .177 & .22. 140 Light Patterns. Most despatches before Jan. 1915. 14 Gun Laying Teachers.
69030-69529	June 1913/Feb. 1914	June 1913/Sept. 1915	All Standard .177 & .22. Most despatches Mid. 1913. 15 Gun Laying Teachers.
69530-70029	July 1913/Feb. 1914	July 1913/April 1915	Mostly Standard .177 & .22. 100 Light Patterns. Standards despatched Winter 1913-14. Light Patterns despatched Winter 1914-15.
70030-70529	Aug. 1913/March 1914	Aug. 1913/July 1914	All Standard Pattern .177 & .22. 1 Light Pattern only.
70530-71029	Sept. 1913/Dec. 1914	Sept. 1913/Dec. 1916	225 Light Patterns despatched up to Dec. 1916. Remainder Standard .177 & .22. Despatched up to Spring 1914.
71030-71529	April/Sept. 1913	May/Dec. 1913	All Standard Patterns.
71530-72029	June/Nov. 1913	June 1913/July 1914	All Standard Patterns Mostly despatched Late 1913.
72030-72529	Sept./Nov. 1913	Sept. 1913/Feb. 1914	Standard .177 & .22 with 3 Light Patterns.
72530-73029	Oct./Nov. 1913	Oct. 1913/Feb. 1914	Standard .177 & .22 with 17 Light Patterns.
73030-73529	Sept. 1913/Dec. 1914	Sept. 1913/Nov. 1916	Majority Light Patterns with 100 Standard .177 & .22. Most despatches Winter 1914/15.
73530-74029	Sept. 1913/March 1914	Sept. 1913/Jan. 1915	Mostly Standard .177 & .22. Despatches up to 1914. 100 Light Patterns despatched up to Jan. 1915.
74030-74529	Oct. 1913/April 1914	Nov. 1913/Nov. 1916	All Standard .177 & .22. Mostly despatched by Oct. 1914.
74530-75029	Nov. 1913/Oct. 1914	Nov. 1913/June 1916	Standard .177 & .22 with 11 Light Patterns. Most despatched by Nov. 1914.
75030-75529	Jan./Aug. 1914	Jan./Nov. 1914	All Standard .177 & .22.
755530-76029	Dec. 1913/Sept. 1914	Dec. 1913/May 1917	1 Light Pattern despatched 1917. Mostly Standard Pattern despatched by End 1914. 88 Light and 1 Junior Pattern.

Serial Numbers	Period of Manufacture	Period of Despatch	Notes
76030-76529	Feb./Dec. 1914	Feb. 1914/Oct. 1917	Mostly Standard .177 & .22 despatched by End 1914. 320 Light Patterns despatched by End of 1917.
76530-77029	July 1914/Sept. 1917	July 1914/Dec. 1917	Standard Patterns despatched up to Dec. 1916. Light Patterns made and despatched Summer 1917. Juvenile Pattern second batch. 112 Numbers not issued.
77030-77529	Nov./Dec. 1913	Nov. 1913/Sept. 1914	Nearly all Juvenile Patterns with few Standards.
77530-78029	Jan./July 1914	Jan. 1914/March 1915	Last 10 Juveniles in second batch then all Standard Patterns.
78030-78529	June/Sept. 1914	June /Oct. 1914	Start of Photo etching cylinders. All Standard .177 & .22. No Numbers issued between 78219 and 78529.
78530-79029	None	None	Not issued.
79030-79529	None	None	Not issued.
79530-80029	April 1914/July 1917	April 1914/July 1917	Mixture of Standard & Light Patterns. Despatched through 1914, 1915, 1916 and 1917. 165 Gun Laying Teachers despatched Mid. 1915. 33 Numbers not issued.
80030-80529	July 1914/Oct. 1917	July 1914/Dec. 1917	16 Light Pattern despatched Mid. 1917. 18 Gun Laying Teachers despatched Mid. 1915. Remaining Standard .177 and .22 despatched 1914, 1915 and 1916. No Numbers issued between 80305-80529.
80530-81029	June/Sept. 1914	June/Nov. 1914	All 3rd batch Juvenile Patterns totalling 200. 300 numbers not issued. Highest recorded Number 80846. Juvenile rifle despatched 27th July 1914.

INDEX OF ILLUSTRATED PLATES

		Page
Frontispiece	'Piled Arms'	2
Plate 1	Lincoln Air Guns 1905	11
Plate 2	Lincoln Stock Marking	12
Plate 3	BSA Stock Marking	13
Plate 4	BSA Breech Plug Top View	14
Plate 5	BSA Breech Plug Right Side	20
Plate 6	BSA Breech Plug Left Side	21
Plate 7	Lincoln Air Rifle First Pattern	22
Plate 8	Early Pattern Trigger Guards	27
Plate 9	Early Pattern Foresight	28
Plate 10	Lincoln Ladies Pattern	29
Plate 11	Improved Model Trigger Guards	30
Plate 12	Lincoln Breech Plug Fastening	34
Plate 13	Breech Plug Retaining Plate	35
Plate 14	Breech Plug Details	36
Plate 15	BSA Air Rifle Improved Model	40
Plate 16	First Military Pattern Advertisement	41
Plate 17	Second Cocking Lever Catch	42
Plate 18	.250″ Model with No. 10 Rearsight	46
Plate 19	'Scout' Magazine Advertisement	47
Plate 20	No. 12 Aperture Rearsight	48

Plate 21   Improved Model D with No. 12 Sight 54

Plate 22   Improved Breech Plug Details 55

Plate 23   Details of Cylinder Locking Screw 56

Plate 24   Improved Model D .22 with No. 19 Sight 60

Plate 25   Sight Details in 1911 BSA Booklet 61

Plate 26   Junior 11¼" Stock Details 62

Plate 27   Junior Air Rifle 65

Plate 28   Cover of 1911 BSA Booklet 66

Plate 29   Details of Side Button Cocking Lever 67

Plate 30   Double Safe Sear Details 68

Plate 31   Double Safe Sear Trigger Block Markings 71

Plate 32   Cocking Lever Marking Details 72

Plate 33   Junior Air Rifles.........................73

Plate 34   Juvenile Air Rifle 74

Plate 35   Juvenile Air Rifle Rearsight 78

Plate 36   Dovetail Fitting Trigger Guard 79

Plate 37   Military Pattern Cylinder Markings 80

Plate 38   Pre Great War Training Rifles.........................83

Plate 39   Pre Great War Training Ammunition 84

Plate 40   Military and Territorial Rifles 85

Plate 41   Military Pattern Air Rifle Third Pattern 86

Plate 42   Military Pattern Air Rifle Third Pattern 90

Plate 43   Military Pattern Cylinder Markings 91

Plate 44   Military Pattern Dummy Bolt 92

Plate 45   Military Pattern Advertisement 1911 95

Plate 46   Military Pattern Advertisement 1913 96

Plate 47   Gun Laying Teacher Land Pattern 97

Plate 48   Gun Laying Teacher Land Pattern 98

Plate 49   BSA Pre War Despatch Ledger 101

Plate 50   Six Sizes of BSA Air Rifles 102

Plate 51   Lincoln Air Rifle Seventh Batch 103

Plate 52   Improved Breech Plug Late Pattern 104

Plate 53   .22 Improved Model D with No. 21 Sight 108

Plate 54   Improved Model D Light Pattern 109

Plate 55   Improved Model D Light & Ordinary Patterns 110

Plate 56   Lincoln Standard and Ladies Patterns 114

Plate 57   Details from 1913 BSA Catalogue 115

Plate 58   Lincoln Air Rifle Ladies Pattern 116

Plate 59   .22 Improved Model D c.1909 120

Plate 60   Details of No. 8 Rearsight 121

Plate 61   No. 8 Backsight on .22 Improved Model D 122

Plate 62   .22 Improved Model D in Wooden Case 128

Plate 63   Lincoln Jeffries Adjustable Breech Plug 129

Plate 64   Lincoln Jeffries Adjusting Breech Plug 130

Plate 65   Lincoln Air Rifle Sectional Diagram 134

Plate 66   Details of BSA Breech Plug 1906 135

Plate 67   George Lincoln Jeffries' Grave 136

Plate 68   George Lincoln Jeffries & Mr. H. Sprawson 139

Plate 69   Cylinder Markings of Gun Laying Teacher 140

Plate 70   Gun Laying Teacher in Holder 141

Plate 71   Drawing of Gun Laying Air Rifle Holder 142

Plate 72   Drawing of Gun Laying Air Rifle 143

Plate 73   Two views of Gun Laying Teacher 144